Transitions

Easy Ways to Adapt to Changes in Your Day

Written by Jeri A. Carroll
Edited by Cindy Iutzi
Illustrated by Cara H. Bradshaw

Teaching & Learning Company
1204 Buchanan St., P.O. Box 10
Carthage, IL 62321-0010

Cover photo by Images and More Photography

ISBN No. 1-57310-070-6

Printing No. 98765432

Teaching & Learning Company
1204 Buchanan St., P.O. Box 10
Carthage, IL 62321-0010

Table of Contents

Dear Teacher or Parent,

I have spent many years in classrooms—as a teacher, as a parent, as an observer and as a supervisor. I have seen many wonderful lessons in which children are thoroughly and thoughtfully engrossed in activities . . . then it becomes time to move to recess, art, music, physical education, the library or lunch. I've watched the children reluctantly leave what they are doing to go where the schedule says they must go. I am reminded of trying to tell someone who's halfway through mowing the lawn that it's time to come in for dinner, or of having to leave to get to the movie on time when the cake needs 10 more minutes in the oven. It's frustrating for an adult. It's no less frustrating for a child. Being sensitive to children's need for completion is just one aspect of creating a successful transition from one activity to the next.

Waiting is another frustration: waiting for the last child to be quiet before reading the story, waiting until everyone has cleaned up before starting the next activity, waiting as roll is called and waiting for the lunch count to be taken. How much time does a child spend sitting and waiting in a given day? If a child waits for one minute five times a day, and is in school for 180 half days, the child will have waited for five full school days! That is a lot of time just sitting and waiting.

Transitions will challenge you to examine your day, to look at those unsettled moments spent moving from one activity to the next, and to realize the lost time spent waiting. You'll find activities for opening the day, for filling empty times, and for quiet and noisy transitions. You may find that providing smoother transitions and filling wait times with purpose will also control some discipline problems.

Make the day more enjoyable for the children and more relaxing for you by using exciting transition activities.

Sincerely,

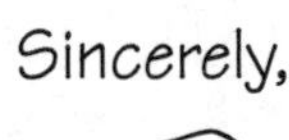

Jeri A. Carroll

Transitions

Smooth Connections

Transitions? What are they? The dictionary defines *transition* as: a passage from one place to another, a movement from one stage to another, and a musical passage leading from one section of a piece to another.

How do transitions fit in education? In the classroom?

A Passage from One Place to Another

A transition occurs as children move from:

- home to school
- the bus to the classroom
- entering the class to circle time
- circle to center time
- center to center
- centers to recess
- recess to restroom
- restroom to class
- class to music
- music to class
- class to lunch
- lunch to recess
- recess to class
- class to PE
- PE to class
- class to after school care
- after school care to home

A Movement from One Stage to Another

A transition occurs as children move from:

- crawling to walking
- being fed to feeding oneself
- day care to preschool
- preschool to kindergarten
- kindergarten to first grade
- first grade to second grade
- the first reading book to the next
- being cared for to caring
- being given to giving
- one skill to the next

A Musical Passage Leading from One Section of a Piece to Another

A transition occurs as children move from:

- one activity to another at a table
- math to reading
- writing to coloring
- reading to workbooks
- working alone to working in pairs

Maybe nothing else happens in life more consistently than transitions.

Overview: An Outline for Easy Reference

Transitions contains information about the kinds of transition situations that are encountered in classrooms. Each section contains a variety of ideas from which to choose. Because no situation is like another, it is up to each teacher to decide which types of transition activities will work in different situations. Making the connections smooth will make the experiences smooth.

DAP: Developmentally Appropriate Activities (pages 10-16)

Use developmentally appropriate practices to help eliminate unnecessary transitions and long periods of time when children are unoccupied or occupied with things of little interest.

The Master Plan (pages 17-20)

Examine what your class might look like in the most ideal situations. See what steps you might take to get to that point.

Schedule Building (pages 21-25)

What does a good schedule look like? How much time should be spent in centers or work stations? How can you make sure everyone gets to do the work and moves from spot to spot in the most unobtrusive way?

Contracts and Reduce Wait Time (pages 26 and 30-33)

Learn ways to eliminate wait time, limit transitions and make necessary transitions smooth. Use contracts to help students organize their time. Schedules, movement cues and monitoring are techniques used to reduce wait time.

Beginnings (page 40)

Learn ways to help children and parents who are new to your school enter the school, become acquainted with the building, familiar with the class routine and comfortable with you.

Examine how to start the school year in ways that allow students to feel safe in the classroom, secure in investigating and exploring, excited about coming to school, and knowledgeable about the rules, routines and responsibilities of being an effective student.

Entering the Classroom (page 50)

Plan new ways for children to become more independent as they enter the room each day and prepare for school. Let children take charge of their own supplies, responsibilities and learning.

Switching Signals (page 71)

Give children warnings about when they must prepare to stop working on one task, get ready to move to the next activity and move smoothly to the next center.

Action Songs (pages 91-95)

Actions songs are a way to signal movement from one activity to another. Action songs also provide an opportunity for controlled physical group activity.

Transition Songs (pages 96-103)

Keep moving. Fill the cleanup time with song. This section provides you with an array of activities you can do while you are cleaning up, getting ready for lunch, preparing for indoor or outdoor recess.

It might even lead you to the creation of your own song.

What Next? (pages 104-128)

Figure out ways to help children know what to do in their spare time or how to get involved in another task. Wait time can only cause problems for a child, for children, and for you. Fill those times with fun-packed fillers. Students may choose something to do from a list of these activities.

School Breaks (pages 129-139)

Provide parents with activities to do during school breaks. Blank pages with borders provide an incentive for children to jot down what they do during these breaks to share with you when they get back.

Summer Fun (pages 140-143)

Children may leave school in the summer thinking that learning stops. Provide some organized ways parents and children can learn together over the summer. Calendars can be sent home at the end of school or mailed monthly.

Make transitions smooth for everyone.

Activities planned and provided for young children should be meaningful, open-ended and require active involvement from the children.

Checklist for Appropriate Practice for Work with 3-Year-Olds

Fine Motor Skills (3-Year-Olds)

- *Time for creative expression and exploration of materials*

Materials Available

- ❑ puzzles
- ❑ pegboards
- ❑ beads to string
- ❑ construction sets
- ❑ crayons
- ❑ paints and brushes
- ❑ markers
- ❑ play dough
- ❑ blunt scissors

Gross Motor Skills (3-Year-Olds)

- *Time and space indoors and outdoors to explore and exercise*

Materials Available

- ❑ various sized balls and beanbags
- ❑ trikes and wagons
- ❑ climbing apparatus
- ❑ balancing boards

Cognition (3-Year-Olds)

- *Time to explore and learn about their environment*
- *Time to be curious*
- *Time to experiment with cause and effect*

Materials Available

- ❑ blocks
- ❑ dramatic play props
- ❑ sand and water table
- ❑ toys for pouring and measuring
- ❑ things to measure
- ❑ scoops
- ❑ toys with knobs and latches
- ❑ toys that open and close
- ❑ toys that can be taken apart (and put back together)
- ❑ bubbles
- ❑ kits
- ❑ seed planting activities

Language
(3-Year-Olds)

- *Time to listen, speak, "read" and "write"*
- *Time to use language to solve problems*
- *Time to use language to learn concepts*

Materials Available

- ❑ books
- ❑ magazines
- ❑ newspapers
- ❑ paper
- ❑ writing implements
- ❑ earphones
- ❑ tapes
- ❑ records

Activities

- ❑ Adults speak clearly and frequently to individual children.
- ❑ Adults respond quickly and appropriately to children.
- ❑ Adults patiently answer the "Why?" and "How come?" questions.
- ❑ Adults respond to repeated questions as children practice conversations.
- ❑ Adults record children's stories.
- ❑ Adults read to children.
- ❑ Children rapidly acquire language.
- ❑ Children experiment with verbal sounds.
- ❑ Children use language to solve problems.
- ❑ Children use language to learn concepts.
- ❑ Children learn nursery rhymes, poems, songs and fingerplays.
- ❑ Children dictate stories.

Checklist for Appropriate Practice for Work with 4 to 5-Year-Olds

- *Experiences meet physical, social, emotional and intellectual needs*
- *Individual differences are expected, accepted and used to design appropriate activities*
- *Interactions and activities promote self-esteem and a positive attitude toward learning*

Environment
(4 to 5-Year-Olds)

- Children learn through interaction with materials and people.
- Children have choices for centers, activities and materials.
- Children are active.
- Children work individually or in small groups most of the time.
- Experiences are concrete and meaningful.

Cognition
(4 to 5-Year-Olds)

- Children develop understanding through interaction and problem solving.
- Meaningful experiences integrate curriculum areas.
- Safe and healthy routines are followed.

Physical Development
(4 to 5-Year-Olds)

- Children use large motor skills daily both indoors and outdoors.

Aesthetic Development
(4 to 5-Year-Olds)

- Children experiment and enjoy various forms of art and music.

Language
(4 to 5-Year-Olds)

- *Time to see that reading and writing are useful*
- *Time to talk with children and adults*
- *Time to use language to solve social problems*

Materials Available

- ❑ books
- ❑ magazines
- ❑ newspapers
- ❑ paper
- ❑ writing implements
- ❑ earphones
- ❑ tapes
- ❑ records

Activities

- ❑ Adults read stories and poems to children.
- ❑ Adults provide field trips for common experiences to talk about.
- ❑ Adults model by using print in meaningful ways.
- ❑ Adults facilitate positive interaction between children.
- ❑ Children "read" stories and poems to adults and other children.
- ❑ Children rapidly acquire language.
- ❑ Children experiment with verbal sounds.
- ❑ Children use language to solve problems.
- ❑ Children use language to learn concepts.
- ❑ Children learn nursery rhymes, poems, songs and fingerplays.
- ❑ Children dictate stories.

Checklist for Appropriate Practice for Work with 5 to 8-Year-Olds

- *Curriculum is designed to meet physical, social, emotional and intellectual needs; to help children learn how to learn and to establish a pattern for lifelong learning.*
- *Individual differences are expected, accepted and used to design appropriate activities. Children are allowed to move at their own pace.*
- *Interactions and activities promote self-esteem and a positive attitude toward learning*

Teaching Strategies
(5 to 8-Year-Olds)

- ☐ Children learn through interaction with materials and people.
- ☐ Curriculum is integrated with learning occurring through projects and learning centers.
- ☐ The curriculum reflects the students' interests and suggestions.
- ☐ Teachers guide children's involvement.
- ☐ Many centers are available so students have choices.
- ☐ Children are encouraged to evaluate their own work.
- ☐ Some work is corrected in small groups where children give each other feedback.
- ☐ Errors are viewed as a necessary and natural part of learning.
- ☐ Students may work alone or in groups.
- ☐ Materials with various textures and shapes are available for manipulation and experimentation.

Language and Literacy (5 to 8-Year-Olds)

- *Children are exposed to a variety of language experiences.*

Activities

- ☐ Children draw, dictate, and/or write.
- ☐ Students play and implement projects.
- ☐ Children make lists of steps to follow.
- ☐ Students discuss what is read.
- ☐ Children prepare class newspapers.
- ☐ Students interview people to obtain information.
- ☐ Children make books.
- ☐ Students listen to and view high-quality films of children's books.
- ☐ Children are read to each day.
- ☐ Students use the school library.
- ☐ Reading skills are taught as needed to individual or small groups of children through enjoyable games and activities.
- ☐ Teachers accept students' invented spelling.
- ☐ Children use literacy skills in other content areas.

Math (5 to 8-Year-Olds)

- *Children use math through exploration, discovery and solving meaningful problems.*

Activities

- ☐ Math activities are integrated with other projects.
- ☐ Math skills are acquired through play, projects and daily living.
- ☐ Many math manipulatives are used.
- ☐ Interesting board and card games are used daily.

Social Studies (5 to 8-Year-Olds)

- *Social studies themes are identified as the focus of activities.*

Activities

- ❑ Children participate in projects and playful activities as they research items in books.
- ❑ Students take field trips.
- ❑ Children interview visitors and speakers.
- ❑ Students work on the social skills of planning, sharing, taking turns and working on committees.
- ❑ Children explore values, learn rules of social living and learn respect of differences through experiences.
- ❑ Cultural experiences in art, music, dance, drama, woodworking and games are provided.

Science (5 to 8-Year-Olds)

- *Discovery science is a major part of the curriculum, building on a child's natural interest.*

Activities

- ❑ Science projects are experimental and exploratory.
- ❑ Science projects build on a child's natural interest in the world.
- ❑ The classroom and outdoors contain plants and pets.
- ❑ Through field trips and projects, students learn to plan, predict, observe, experiment and verify.

Other Curriculum Areas (5 to 8-Year-Olds)

Activities

- ❑ Meaningful health and safety projects enable children to learn about personal health and safety.
- ❑ Art, music, movement, woodworking, drama and dance are integrated into meaningful experiences and projects. Specialists work with classroom teachers.
- ❑ Multicultural and nonsexist activities and materials are available.
- ❑ Outdoor activity allows for gross motor development and appropriate expression.

To see if the day is well planned for young children, refer to the publication of the National Association for the Education of Young Children, *Developmentally Appropriate Practice in Early Childhood Programs Serving Children from Birth Through Age 8* (Bredekamp, 1987) available through the NAEYC offices: 1509 16th Street, N.W., Washington, D.C. 20036-1426 (1-800-424-2460).

The Master Plan

To make transitions smooth, visualize what the class should ultimately look like. Set a goal for a smoothly running classroom by the fifth week of school. Use the first four weeks to map out strategies to meet the goal.

In planning, remember the consensus values of honesty, respect, responsibility, compassion, self-discipline, perseverance and giving. (*The Basic School*, Ernest Boyer, The Carnegie Foundation for the Advancement of Teaching, 1995). Weave those values into expectations for the classroom.

Fifth Week of School: The Goal

As children enter the classroom, they check their responsibilities for the day, put things they have brought from home in appropriate places and get involved in the first activity of the day. Bring them together to share their connections from the day before (how they connect what they have learned to their life away from school) and plan for the new day. After an information giving-gathering-getting session, children may choose from 9 to12 centers in the room while individual and group conferences take place with children in reading, writing or math. A break for PE or recess allows planned and sequenced development of gross motor skills and group participation in games.

Snacks and lunch are social as well as nutritional. Children return for connections from the morning's activities to their out-of-class time, the information giving-gathering-getting session and learning centers. Formal closure evaluates what has been done that day, how connections might be made during the time away from school and what will happen the next day. Everyone leaves excited about the day they have had and the day to come.

To achieve "The Goal," begin at the beginning-Week 1.

Week 1: Structure Promotes Safety and Security

Children enter a strange room with all their belongings. They don't know where to go, what is in store for them, who will be there or how their basic needs will be met. It is important to establish safety and security early, and that is most often done through structure and close contact.

During the first week, structure the class. Children are asked to enter, take off coats and sit on the carpet to play with something that is put out for them. When everyone is seated, take attendance, read a story, and move quickly to centers.

Each center has only one set of materials available on the first day. Every day add an additional set. Demonstrate materials at the centers or at circle time before children go to the centers. Rotate children through centers briefly, with only enough time for initial investigation of materials. Change groups each day to see which children work best together. Remember, the goal in the first week is for children to feel safe and secure, not to gain a lot of information.

Conduct group tours of the building and grounds daily to acclimate the children in places other than their own classroom. Play time outside is in a small space with only one classroom at a time.

Circle times are active with the teacher as leader. Tell or read and lead songs that are familiar to the children.

Observe, monitor, direct and redirect during the first week. Little teaching occurs when a teacher's class time is spent as group organizer.

Establish simple classroom rules for safety and group functioning. Some examples are: walk in the classroom; watch where you are going; stay with your group; keep the teacher in sight; be nice to your friends. Establish rules, teach the rules to the children and remind them of the rules throughout the day using the exact words and reinforce the rules. Watch to see that the class is following the rules.

Week 2: A Sense of Belonging Fosters Responsibilities

In the second week, children should begin to feel safe and secure. Reduce the high structure of the first week by giving a little more freedom and responsibility to the children. When they come into the classroom, they may be told to get something to work with on the carpet or to go there and talk with friends.

Circle times are a bit longer, although they continue to be active.

Increase the length of center times. Most of the materials were introduced in the first week so that each center now has several sets of materials. Continue to assign groups to centers. The amount of time spent in centers is directly related to how long the children stay active at the center before becoming inactive. Watch for inactivity and redirect children within the center if possible. When several children get restless, it is time to rotate. Length of stay in each center ranges from 8 to 10 minutes. Remind students that they are responsible for the care and maintenance of materials, space and equipment.

In the second week students begin to feel as if they belong together. They look out for themselves and each other. Some might suggest a group name for the class and decorations to match.

Rules might be broken, usually unintentionally. The children just forget them. Try to be kind, but use immediate redirection strategies. However, if simple redirection is not enough, establish consequences. Be sure to follow through with consequences immediately, not after three to four reminders.

Week 3: Working Together, Learning Problem Solving

By the third week, children feel safer and more secure, more a part of the group and somewhat responsible. The teacher's first two weeks have been spent in observation, monitoring and redirecting. This continues, but now social or academic problem resolution can begin. Continue to make children feel safe and secure, even if it is necessary to enter their work space and work or play activities. Always guide, allow exploration or right and wrong solutions and encourage safe risk taking. Do not correct, reprimand and sanction.

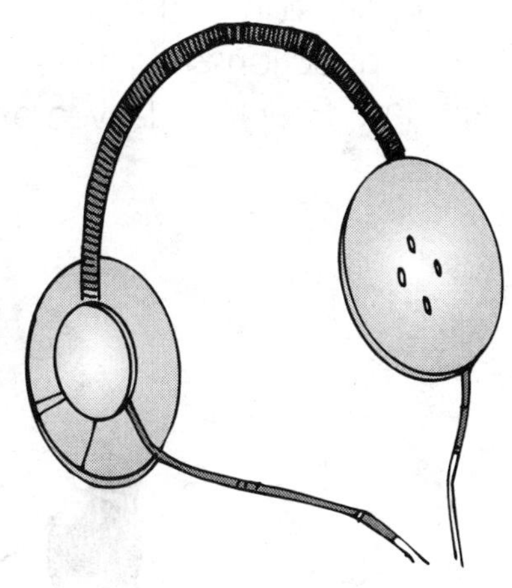

These observations are not only to encourage problem solving, but to see what each child can do and may be ready to learn. Recording these observations takes time. This is the week for you to record observations if you have not already started.

When children enter the classroom, they automatically put their things away and choose an activity to get involved in. Don't ask them to sit on the carpet or talk with friends, but ask them to go right to centers and get to "work" (play). Allow children to choose their work area and the length of time they want to play there. Circle times are well planned, but interject them into the schedule as needed or when appropriate. Intensive work is not interrupted.

Week 4: Conferencing, Instructioning and Evaluating

The ultimate goal is getting closer. Children enter the room and get to work. Move them when needed if they don't move themselves. There is time to conference with children in skill areas that need development. Those skill areas change with time. Young children may need help exploring the use of crayons, markers and pencils. Other children may need help counting objects (setting the table in housekeeping) while older children may need help adding two-digit numbers. Because they feel safe and secure, have a sense of belonging and have been guided in problem solving, they are deeply engrossed in the activities at the centers. The result is time for the teacher to work with individual children that have needs. Individual goals may be set, and tasks may be decided upon. As the child performs the tasks, the teacher and child can evaluate responsibilities.

Lunch break allows for out-of-the-class socialization and nutrition. The children return for connections from the morning's activities to the out-of-class time, an information giving-gathering-getting session and learning centers. Formal closure looks at what has been done that day, how connections might be made during the time away from school and what will happen the next day. Everyone leaves excited about the day they have had and the day to come.

Schedule Building

Schedules

Examples of structure for work and play periods are included in this section. Structure suggestions range from the *most* structured (which will cause the most problems with keeping students on task and with transitions) to the *least* structured (which may be a teacher's personal goal set for the end of the year, if the first part of the year was extremely structured).

- Centers: Assigned and Rotated
- Work Times: Curriculum Directed
- Centers: Teacher Selected and Free Choice Activities
- Centers: Integrated Curriculum

Schedules for young children are structured enough to provide security, allow the child to know what is going to happen next and are flexible enough to meet the needs of various children at various times. Short, chopped-up periods of time do not allow children the depth of involvement that they need. Long extended, periods of time spent sitting and taking turns will only cause problems.

As children enter the room, give them time to adjust to the transition from home to school. They should know what is expected. They are allowed to socialize and must be ready to start the day's activities within a short time. Time elapsed from the start of school to the end of this activity should be five to10 minutes, depending on the size of the group.

Children need time to get focused for the day. Some may remember from the day before where they want to start. Others need more direction. A group time at the beginning of the day to get focused helps most children. However, extended circle times which involve calendar, weather, counting, sequencing, milk count, attendance, etc., will only cause problems. This transition will not be smooth. Circle time should be over in 10 minutes or less.

Children should get right to work or play. About eight to 12 stations or centers provide ample opportunities for twenty-four children to have variety, choice and meaningful experiences in the classroom. Areas for reading, writing, listening, playing, building, constructing, creating, solving, predicting, testing, moving and singing, allow for integrated exploration of various themes and topics.

Centers: Assigned and Rotated

Determine the number of children in the classroom and the number of centers available. Divide children into even groups. Set up a master schedule for the week that allows rotation to all centers. Try to allow at least 30 minutes per center.

Theoretically this does not allow for children's interest, choice, variety, etc. This method allows every child to experience every center each week, but groups remain the same, children cannot leave when they are finished or stay if they aren't. Because they cannot choose which center to go to, a variety of activities must be presented at each center.

	Mon.		Tues.		Wed.		Thurs.		Fri.	
	9:30	10:00	9:30	10:00	9:30	10:00	9:30	10:00	9:30	10:00
Alex	R	A	W	P	Sc	Sa	L	GM	M	C
Anwar	R	A	W	P	Sc	Sa	L	GM	M	C
Bonnie	R	A	W	P	Sc	Sa	L	GM	M	C
Brad	R	A	W	P	Sc	Sa	L	GM	M	C
Callie	W	P	Sc	Sa	L	GM	M	C	R	A
Cheyenne	W	P	Sc	Sa	L	GM	M	C	R	A
Dominick	W	P	Sc	Sa	L	GM	M	C	R	A
Donna	W	P	Sc	Sa	L	GM	M	C	R	A
Eduardo	S	Sa	L	GM	M	C	R	A	W	P
Ellie	S	Sa	L	GM	M	C	R	A	W	P
Fran	S	Sa	L	GM	M	C	R	A	W	P
Frank	S	Sa	L	GM	M	C	R	A	W	P

A–Art
C–Crafts
GM–Gross Motor
L–Listening
M–Math
P–Puzzles
R–Reading
Sc–Science
Sa–Sand
W–Writing

Work Times: Curriculum Directed

In the early grades of elementary school, teachers are often guided by the curriculum selected for the grade. The day seems to be directed by the curriculum. Teachers work hard to make sure all the material is covered.

Children meet curriculum requirements, but subjects are isolated and disjointed, not integrated and meaningful.

	8:00	8:30	10:00	10:30	11:30	1:00	2:00	3:00
Monday	O At LC PD	L R W Re	Rc Rs Wa	M	S Lu Rc SR	Li	Sc	SS
Tuesday	O At LC PD	L R W Re	Rc Rs Wa	M	S Lu Rc SR	PE	Sc	SS
Wednesday	O At LC PD	L R W Re	Rc Rs Wa	M	S Lu Rc SR	Mu	Sc	SS
Thursday	O At LC PD	L R W Re	Rc Rs Wa	M	S Lu Rc SR	PE	H	SS
Friday	O At LC PD	L R W Re	Rc Rs Wa	M	S Lu Rc SR	Ar	H	SS

At–Attendance
Ar–Art
H–Health
L–Language
LC–Lunch Count
Li–Library
Lu–Lunch
M–Math
Mu–Music
O–Opening
PD–Plan Day
PE–Physical Education
R–Reading
Re–Research
Rs–Restroom
Rc–Recess
Sc–Science
S–Story
SS–Social Studies
SR–Silent Reading
Wa–Water
W–Writing

Centers: Teacher Selected and Free Choice Activities (FCA)

Provide four to five activity centers each week where children choose from three to five developmentally appropriate activities to complete. Each student goes to one center a day for a specific amount of time. Adjust time to the children, starting with at least 10 minutes for the four-year-olds. At the end of a specific time, children may choose to stay where they are or go to another center. The only rule governing this schedule is that only children assigned to a center may be at the center. (The children are really not taking charge of their education, because teachers select the activities for placement in the centers and room.)

Using this process, children perform specific activities that may be skill or theme specific. Children try new things in a safe environment with friends there to guide or help them. They also have a free choice activity (FCA).

	Mon. (1 hr.)		Tues. (1 hr.)		Wed. (1 hr.)		Thurs. (1 hr.)		Fri. (1 hr.)	
	9:30	9:40	9:30	9:40	9:30	9:40	9:30	9:40	9:30	9:40
Alex	L	FCA	W	FCA	S	FCA	R	FCA	M	FCA
Anwar	L	FCA	W	FCA	S	FCA	R	FCA	M	FCA
Bonnie	L	FCA	W	FCA	S	FCA	R	FCA	M	FCA
Brad	L	FCA	W	FCA	S	FCA	R	FCA	M	FCA
Callie	W	FCA	S	FCA	L	FCA	M	FCA	R	FCA
Cheyenne	W	FCA	S	FCA	L	FCA	M	FCA	R	FCA
Dominick	W	FCA	S	FCA	L	FCA	M	FCA	R	FCA
Donna	W	FCA	S	FCA	L	FCA	M	FCA	R	FCA
Eduardo	S	FCA	L	FCA	M	FCA	R	FCA	W	FCA
Ellie	S	FCA	L	FCA	M	FCA	R	FCA	W	FCA
Fran	S	FCA	L	FCA	M	FCA	R	FCA	W	FCA
Frank	S	FCA	L	FCA	M	FCA	R	A	W	P

A–Art
FCA–Free Choice Activity
L–Listening
M–Math
P–Puzzles
R–Reading
S–Science
W–Writing

Centers: Integrated Curriculum

The teacher plans integrated themes based on student interest and need. Work stations include necessary equipment, reference materials and supplies. Students contract to work on specific skills and to learn specific objectives. Work is documented in student portfolios with teacher-student conferences held one to three times weekly or as needed, during the work station time.

With this method, children are allowed extended work times to get involved with contracted subjects or skills. The teacher is free to work with individual children and small groups to determine what skills and concepts need to be addressed in the large group times. The transition at the beginning of the day allows children to enter the room and get right to work, allowing for few disruptions.

8:00	10:00	10:30	11:00	12:00	1:00	3:00
Children enter and go to work stations	Group Time Review or work completed	Break	Teacher-guided skill instruction or information seeking	Lunch Recess	Students return to work stations	Large group plans for next day
Teacher guides children to stations and with skills as needed		Children enter and go to work stations			Teacher guides and instructs	

Contracts

Use contracts with children so they know what is expected of them when a lesson or project is completed. With very young children, use a set of pictures like those on pages 27 and 28. This section provides several suggestions for contracts.

Have children plan ahead of time what it is they are going to do. They check it off when it is complete and move on to the next job.

Assign some activities and let children choose others.

Assign all activities for those who show they need extensive or detailed directions. Try to guide them to make their own decisions.

Glue pictures on the card to show what to do today.

My plans for the day.

____________________ name

____________________ date

Journal Writing

Math

Reading

Puzzles

Gross Motor

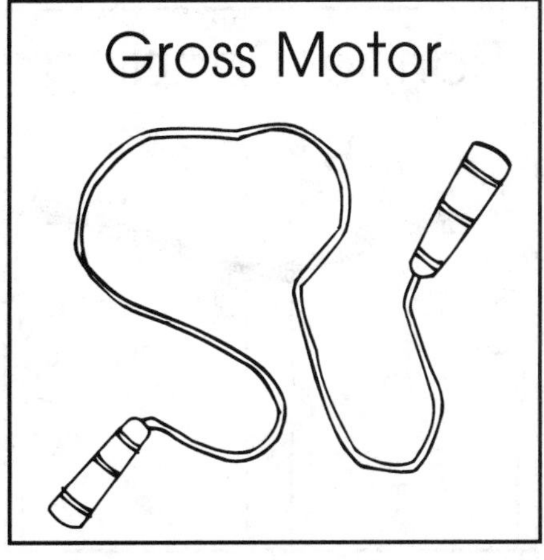

Creative Writing

Art

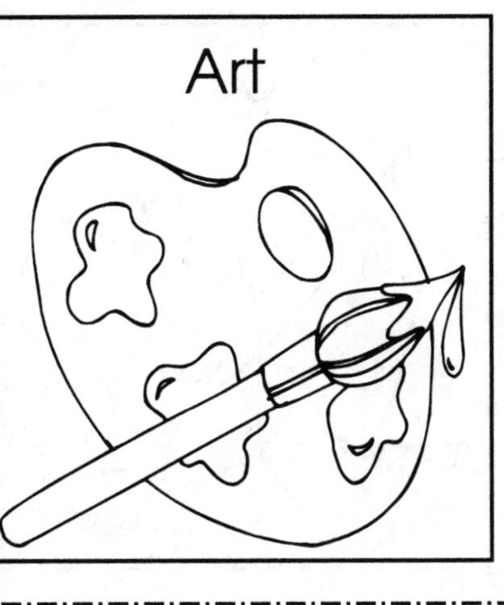

Large Blocks

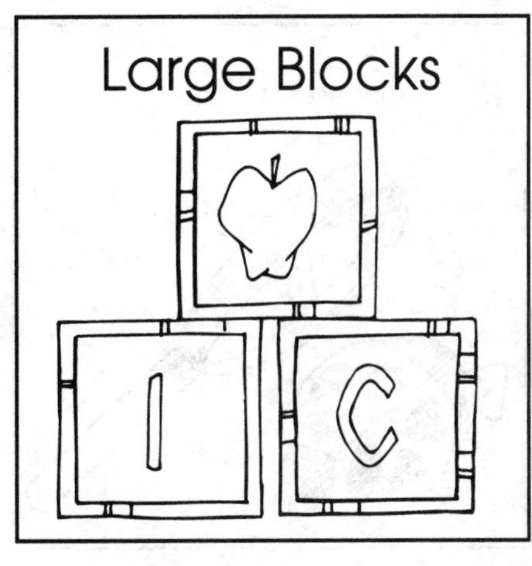

Small Blocks

Library

House

Math

Listening

Sand Table

Water Table

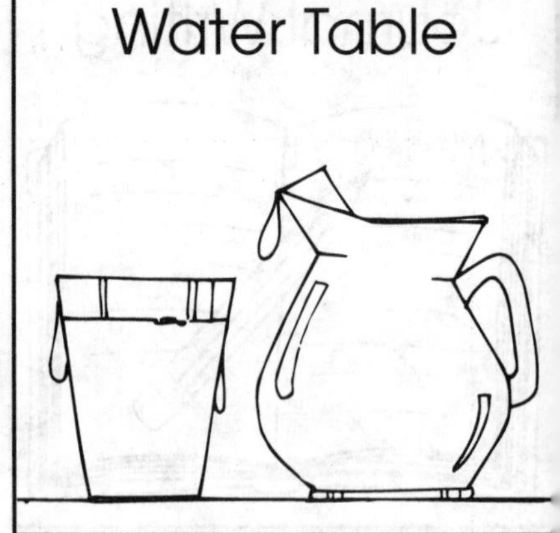

Free Choice

Partner Reading

Teacher Assisted

Teacher Conference

Science

Health

PE

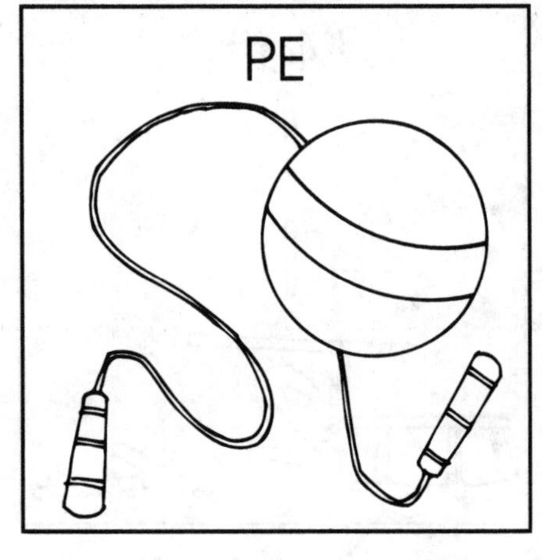

Music

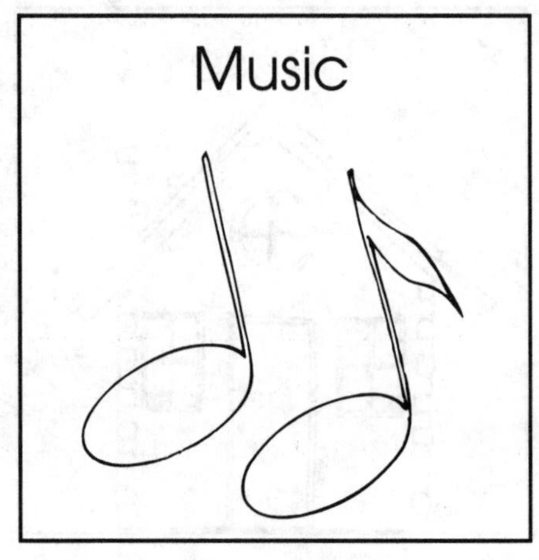

Fine Motor

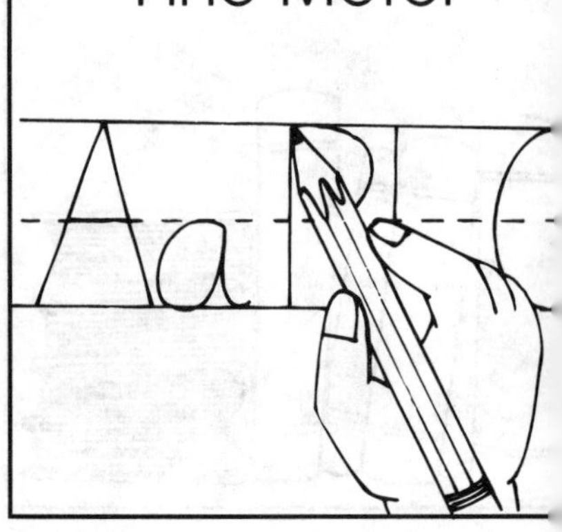

Plans for the Week of ______________________

Subject	Monday	Tuesday	Wednesday	Thursday	Friday

Teachers provide structured assignments for children each day in selected subjects. As students finish the assignment, they make a check in the appropriate box. When assignments are finished, students may attend free choice centers in the classroom.

Reduce Wait Time

Several times throughout the day children must go from one place to another. These times, if not well planned, can cause confusion, make children wait and encourage misbehavior. Make the children responsible so the teacher does not have to take control. Use these strategies:

Schedules

Post the schedule so children know what to do now, next and throughout the day. The schedule may change throughout the year, especially during the first few weeks.

Name					
Alisa					
Jose					
Ruth					
Mike					
Tanisha					
Jana					
Jill					
Tim					

Movement

Make cues to move from one activity to the next clear, whether children are allowed to move freely or only when scheduled.

Monitoring Work

Be able to know at a glance whether everyone is working successfully on task or if someone needs assistance.

Preparation for Today

Children should be prepared for what is going to happen during the day. Preparation can be accomplished by discussing the previous day, "enter and check," bulletin board, sharing table and class opening.

Preparation for Tomorrow

Prepare children for tomorrow at the end of today. This helps students get excited about what is planned for tomorrow. Use the experience cards to show what they have done today. Then rearrange the cards for tomorrow as part of today's closing activities. This also helps children answer the question, "What did you do in school today?"

Working Partnerships

Allow children to work closely with others, in small groups or independently. As time goes along their ability to do each should improve. However, they may favor one type of working relationship over another.

Schedule Ideas

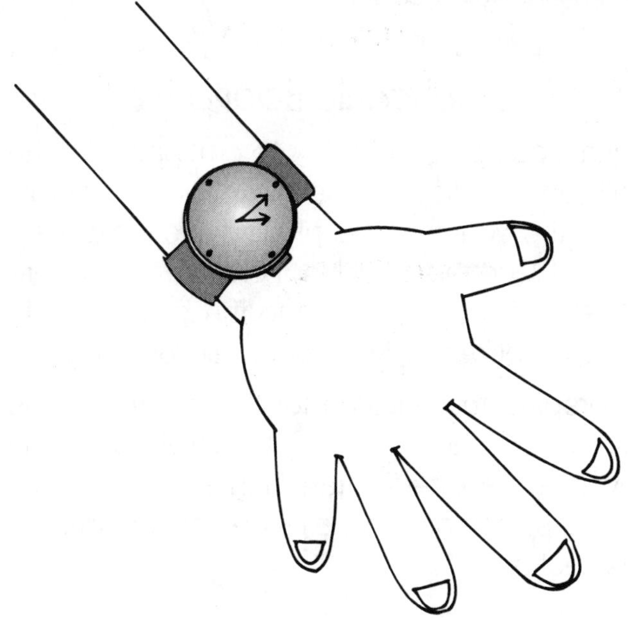

Scheduling Time

Young children need uninterrupted times for meaningful work experiences. Clumps of work time should be provided that are 45 to 60 minutes in length with some free choice activities within that time. This allows children time to practice things they already know how to do and to meet mentally and physically challenging activities in a safe and supportive environment. Children should also have some say about the amount of time they spend on activities. If necessary, allow children to continue activities from one time to the next and even one day to the next.

Consistency in Schedules

Young children require stability within their environment. They need some consistency in their schedules. Schedules need to be predictable. When changes occur, teachers should prepare children for the changes.

Balance in Schedules

Schedules need a balance of mentally active times, physically active times and quiet times.

Experience Cards

Illustrated cards are on pages 34 to 39 or you may wish to photograph children engaged in various experiences in your classroom: puzzles, dramatic play, blocks, construction, art, easel, reading, spelling, math, music, physical education, health, social studies, library, language, writing, etc. Place the photographs in plastic snapshot covers and label each photo with a one-word caption.

Schedule Board

Cut a piece of 4" x 6" (10 x 15 cm) paper for the children to display their experience cards. Allow the width of the photo for each experience. Place the board in a chalk tray. Adhere a piece of magnetic tape to the board and to the back of each plastic photo envelope.

To prepare the children for the day, place the experience cards in order of activities for the day. Save space for transition activities which can be selected from the movement activities in this section.

In the News

Cover a bulletin board with old newspapers. Write *In the News* at the top. Post important school events on the bulletin board in ways that your children can "read" them.

Sharing Table

Have a special spot where children can place work they have finished or special things they want to show others. Children may check the table periodically during the week.

Enter and Check

As children enter the classroom, they check the schedule board for the day's activities. By using this method, students enter the class, do the basic preparation activities and get right to work. The large group times can be scheduled later in the day when it is necessary to fill in some time.

Class Opening

Many people feel it is important to gather children together first thing in the morning for opening "exercises." But these "exercises" require very little movement from children. In fact, they require children to sit next to each other, not talk, be still and listen (all of which go against the grain of most children when they return to their classmates each day). This time should be limited and should also require as much participation of each child as possible. Eliminate most calendar helpers, weather helpers, attendance counters, etc., where one child is active while the other 10 to 20 sit waiting. (Remember that wait time only leads to misbehavior.)

Welcome children to school ("I'm so glad to see you all today.") and tell them they are going to have a great time ("We are going to be working on some very exciting things today."). Tell them what special things are planned ("Today is the day we go to the library for animal books.") and how the day's events will occur ("And you can tell by the schedule board what the day looks like. Read it with me.").

Reduce Wait Time
Math
0 0 0
0 0
2 0
3
1
+2
3

Reduce Wait Time
Science

Reduce Wait Time
Reading

Reduce Wait Time
Writing

Listening Center

Reduce Wait Time

Language Arts

Puzzles

Reduce Wait Time

Social Studies

Health
Reduce Wait Time
Healthy
foods

Art
Reduce Wait Time

Music
Reduce Wait Time

Library
Reduce Wait Time

Foreign Language

Reduce Wait Time

Gross Motor Center

Centers

Reduce Wait Time

Free Choice

Reduce Wait Time

Opening

Reduce Wait Time

Closing

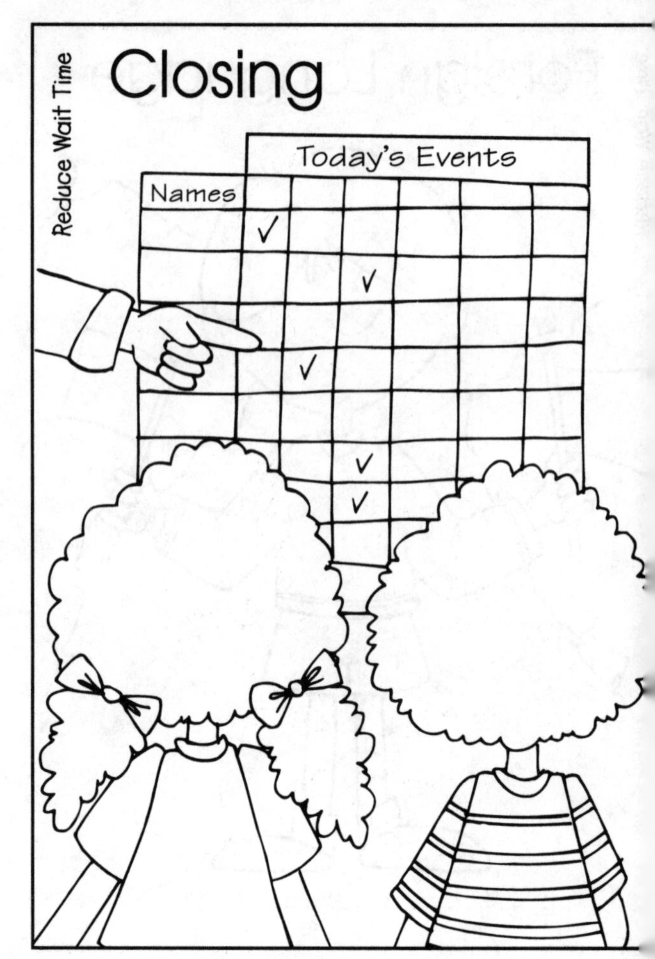

Reduce Wait Time

Restroom

Reduce Wait Time

Lunch

Recess

Reduce Wait Time

Rest

Buddy Reading

Reduce Wait Time

Sustained Silent Reading

Beginnings

Get children off to the right start with a smooth transition into the classroom.

NAEYC (National Association for the Education of Young Children) suggests four strategies to teachers:

- Provide developmentally appropriate curriculum for all age levels in all educational settings.
- There should be ongoing communications and cooperation between staff in different programs. Teachers should visit schools that are sending students to them and should visit schools where they may be sending students.
- Parents should be involved in the transitions. Teachers need to inform parents of their expectations and should listen to parents' concern for their children (see Parent Information Activities).
- Prepare children for transition to the next level by allowing visits to the new classroom and by introducing them to the new teacher (see activities below). If all else fails, a letter or phone call is suggested (see Activities of Welcome).

These good beginnings can actually start with children visiting the classroom in the spring before they begin school. Follow the visits with letters of welcome in the summer. Home visits before school or during school allow the teacher and families to feel more comfortable with one another. Great first day and first week activities help children make the transition to school and to the classroom.

Spring Visits

One Class in Each Grade: Ready for the Next Year

If the class is in a building that has only one class for each grade, work closely with the teacher above or below the grade to make sure things go smoothly for the following year. A lower grade teacher should ask the upper grade teacher at the beginning of the year to save one or two of the worksheets or activities done during the first week. During the last weeks of the school year, introduce children to the type of work that the next year's teacher will be doing.

One Class in Each Grade: Peer Tutoring

Pair up the children in one grade with the children in the next grade. Have the children in the upper grade come to lower grade to work with and read to the children throughout the year. In the spring, switch. Let the lower grade go to the upper grade to read and work.

Story Time

Invite the teacher that the children will most likely have next year to read to them during the teacher's break time. If this is not possible, switch with the teacher and while that teacher reads to the class, visit with last year's children. If there is more than one teacher, set up a schedule so all are able to visit at least once.

Come to My Garden

The kindergarten teacher should invite the preschoolers to "Come to My Garden." (Kindergarten actually means "garden of children.") Ask children in the school to identify potential kindergarten students. Send a note to these students. Also send letters or notes to nearby preschools.

(Note: This activity can easily be adapted to suit other grade levels.)

Come to My Garden

The children of

_______________________________'s
teacher's name

class invite you to visit on

____
day

____
month

____
year

from ____________ to ____________.

We'll have a special gift for you.

We've all signed this invitation.
Do you know any of us?

See you soon.

Visit Day

Ahead of Time: Name Tags

Ask the class to decorate borders around self-adhesive name tags. Have them make enough for the new children, accompanying adults, classmates and the teacher. The class and teacher should put their tags on before the "party." As new students enter the door, make a name tag for each one.

Ahead of Time: Place Mats

Ask students to make and decorate place mats with pictures of things they have done during the school year. Laminate the place mats for use during the refreshment period. Assign children to pass them out to visitors on the day of the visit.

Ahead of Time: Rhymes, Songs and Action Games

Prepare students by going through the rhymes, songs and action games that they know. Ask them to select by picture (see pages 74-94) the ones they think the new children will know.

Ahead of Time: Snacks

Make the day's snacks with the class. Prepare enough for them, the new student, the new student's family and the teacher. Try recipes from favorite cookbooks or request contributions from parents.

Assign children to hand out snacks on the day of the visit and to set up a snack table.

Ahead of Time: Gifts

Prepare or purchase a small gift for each child to take home. Try a flower, a craft stick picture frame, a decorated juice can as a crayon or pencil holder. Set up a gift table ahead of time.

At the Door

A current student's parent should greet visiting families and children at the door while the teacher is in the circle area. Provide each person with a name tag. Pair the new family and child with a student. If a student knows some of the new families and students, pair them with those people. The transition will be smoother for everyone. Children who are very shy should be paired first with a person from their class and then with an incoming pair. Or assign shy children special tasks such as handing out place mats, choosing songs, etc.

Chairs and Forms for Families

Place chairs around the room at various spots for adults to sit in as they observe. If there are forms that they need to fill out, provide a packet and pencils at each chair so they may complete the information while they are there.

Welcome Letter to Families

Provide a welcome letter to families as they come in. This letter will substitute for a personal introduction and greeting. The teacher is usually busy monitoring students and visiting children. Be personable in the letter and provide a schedule of the visit (see below).

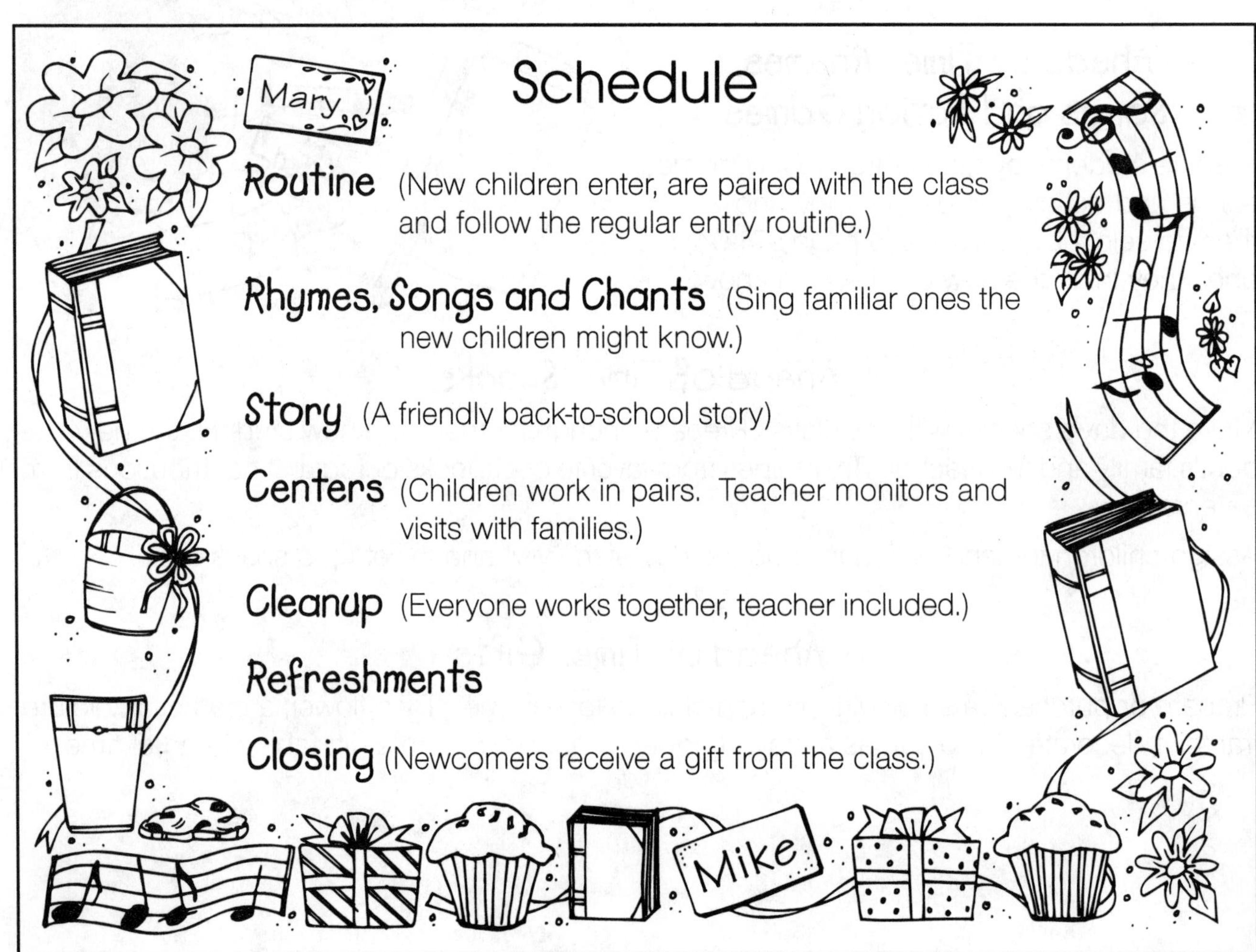

Routine

As children are paired with newcomers, have them follow the same routine for entering the room as on a normal day. Have students tell the newcomers each of the things they do as they come in the room (hang up their coats, put their lunch boxes away, unpack their backpacks, etc.). They should end up sitting at the circle area with the teacher.

Rhymes, Songs and Chants

As the children come to the circle area, begin with familiar rhymes, songs and action games that the class has selected ahead of time. If there are information sheets for the parents to fill out about their children, ask them which rhymes, songs and chants their children know.

Back to School Story

Read a story about school to the children. Try *Will I Have a Friend?* or *Grover Goes to School.*

Centers

Assign the children to centers to work much the same way as they would on a normal day. Students should take their partner with them and demonstrate how to do the various activities. At cleanup time, encourage all the children to work together so snacks can be served.

Snacks

Students should serve the new children, with the place mat and snacks. Then students may return to the snack table and get snacks for the adult visitors. Finally, they serve themselves and return to sit and eat.

Gifts

Have all children return to the circle. Thank them and their families for sharing the day with the class. Have students choose a gift from the gift table and give it to their new friend.

Home Visits

Everyone is a bit anxious about doing things for the first time. Young children are no different. Help them look forward to entering the classroom for the first time by making it familiar ahead of time. Home visits are an excellent way to meet children and families. However, if home visits are not possible, be sure to send a letter of welcome and an invitation to the classroom.

Letters of Introduction and Welcome

Letter to the Children

Teachers should introduce themselves to prospective students through a personal letter. Include information about the teacher, the classroom and scheduled events for the first day and first week. Send something from the classroom for the new students to bring with them on the first day. (See suggestions below.)

Print the note to children. Copy enough for all the children in the class to have one. Make some extras for new children who might come in during the year. Print the name of each child on the letter of introduction.

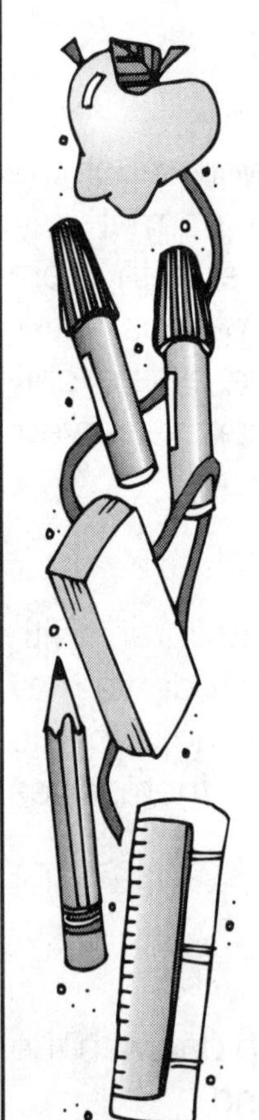

Dear _________________,

My name is Mrs. Carroll. I will be your teacher in second grade at Woodland School. We will be on the first floor in room 104.

I hope you have had a fun summer. I did. I went to the East Coast with my two girls, Callie and Molly, to visit their Aunt Jackie, Uncle Dan, Aunt Mary and Uncle Jack. We stayed in Washington, D.C., and Mt. Eagle, Pennsylvania. I have many of photographs to show you and stories to tell. What did you do this summer?

When you come to school, I want you to look for your new class pet. He's really excited to see you. We'll have to think of a good name for him. Guess what he is!

Please bring the enclosed puzzle piece with you on the first day and a picture of yourself, too. Don't forget your school supplies either.

See you soon!

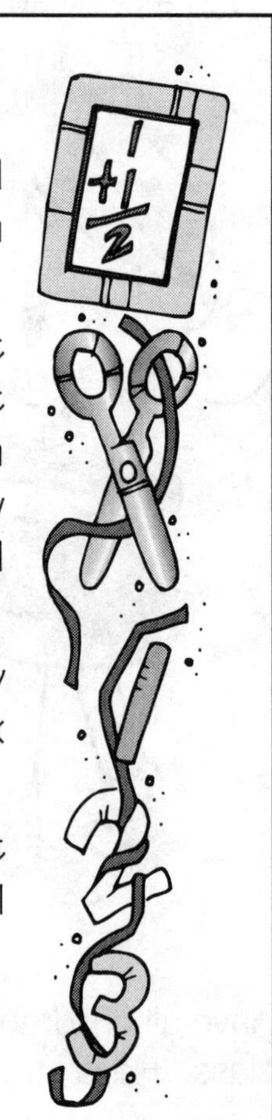

Hide and Seek

The welcome note should tell the children about something they are to look for when they get to the classroom. It might be a puzzle, computer, sand table, class pet, etc.

A Piece of the Puzzle

Cover a small bulletin board with butcher paper. Cut the paper into enough puzzle shapes for each child to have one piece. Number the pieces on the back to show where they belong when the puzzle is put back together.

Also ask each child to bring a picture of himself. Rubber cement the picture to the butcher paper puzzle piece. Work with the children to put the puzzle together on the bulletin board.

Everyone Is Needed

Purchase two puzzles with approximately the same number of pieces as children in the classroom. Send a piece of the puzzle in the welcome letter and ask children to bring it with them on the first day of school. Put the puzzle together to show that to make a good picture, everyone is needed.

Additional puzzle pieces may be given to the principal, director, teacher, janitor, secretary, social service worker, nurse, other teachers, etc. Ask these people to drop in throughout the day to help make the puzzle complete. This will help the children see that everyone else in the school is needed, too.

The second puzzle is to assure that if someone doesn't bring their piece to school there is one to give them. If the second puzzle's pieces aren't needed, put them at a free choice station.

Sample Welcome Letters

These letters are not meant to be photocopied and mailed. Handwrite the letters on school letterhead or within some of the artistic borders that are provided in this book.

(See pages 130-139.)

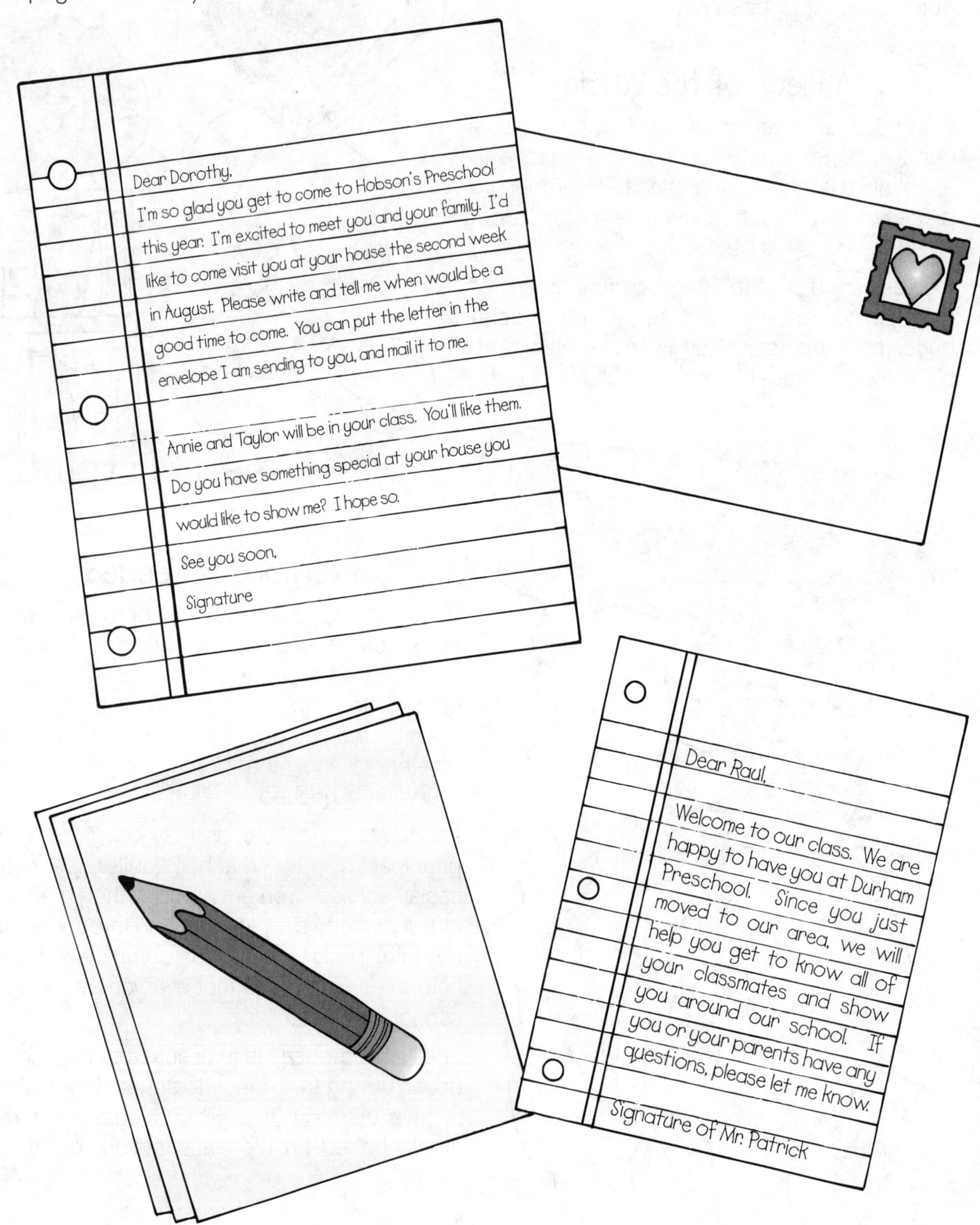

Dear Dorothy,

I'm so glad you get to come to Hobson's Preschool this year. I'm excited to meet you and your family. I'd like to come visit you at your house the second week in August. Please write and tell me when would be a good time to come. You can put the letter in the envelope I am sending to you, and mail it to me.

Annie and Taylor will be in your class. You'll like them. Do you have something special at your house you would like to show me? I hope so.

See you soon,

Signature

Dear Raul,

Welcome to our class. We are happy to have you at Durham Preschool. Since you just moved to our area, we will help you get to know all of your classmates and show you around our school. If you or your parents have any questions, please let me know.

Signature of Mr. Patrick

Sample Welcome Letters

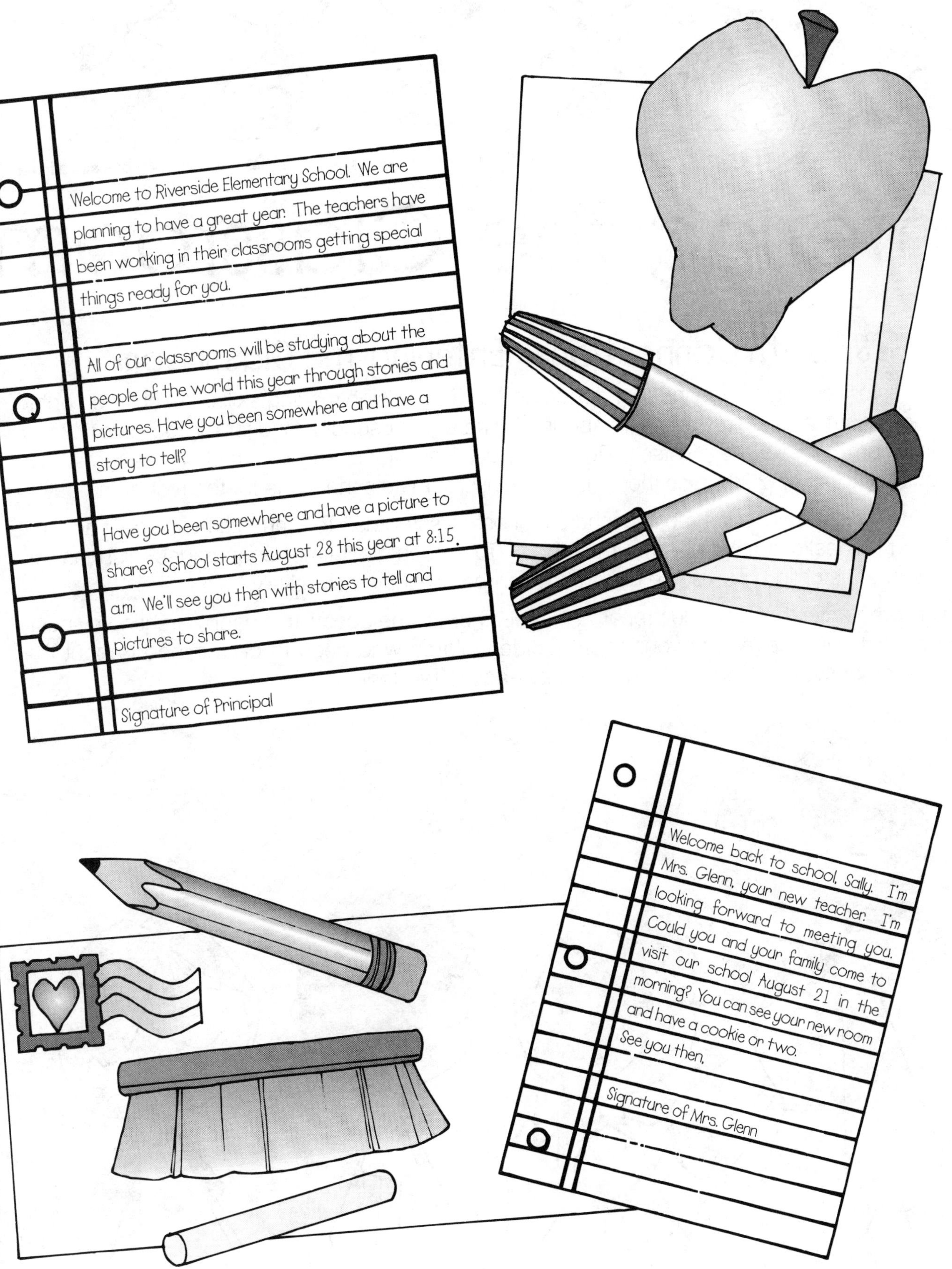
Welcome to Riverside Elementary School. We are planning to have a great year. The teachers have been working in their classrooms getting special things ready for you.

All of our classrooms will be studying about the people of the world this year through stories and pictures. Have you been somewhere and have a story to tell?

Have you been somewhere and have a picture to share? School starts August 28 this year at 8:15 a.m. We'll see you then with stories to tell and pictures to share.

Signature of Principal

Welcome back to school, Sally. I'm Mrs. Glenn, your new teacher. I'm looking forward to meeting you. Could you and your family come to visit our school August 21 in the morning? You can see your new room and have a cookie or two. See you then.

Signature of Mrs. Glenn

Entering the Classroom

Smooth Connections: Entering the Classroom

Responsibilities encourage independence and good decision-making skills. As children enter the classroom, they are moving from about 25 different households and family societies into the schoolroom, a mini society in itself. Rules change. Behavior changes. Children change. What teachers expect of children as they enter the classroom sets the stage for the rest of the day.

Many tasks are required of most teachers in most classrooms. Too much time is spent accomplishing the tasks, so that children must wait. Too much "wait time" encourages misbehavior. "Wait time" as children enter the classroom can be eliminated creatively.

As children enter the room, be prepared to meet them at the door with a happy greeting by posting the following page near your door. Guide children who need to be reminded about the sequence of events upon entering, to what needs to be done.

Sayings for a Good Beginning

Use a child's name with each statement.

Picture Cue Cards

Place the cue cards (pages 52-55) in sequential order in the front of the room. The cards tell children what they must do when they first enter the room. The order in which they are placed will depend on the room's arrangement, the children's age and what is happening in the room in general.

Entering the Classroom

Enter room.

Entering the Classroom

Put lunches away.

Entering the Classroom

Hang up coats.

Entering the Classroom

Check library books

Sharpen pencils.

Use the restroom.

Entering the Classroom

Entering the Classroom

Sign in.

Register for lunch.

Entering the Classroom

Entering the Classroom

Register for milk.

Entering the Classroom

Finish homework.

Entering the Classroom

Put name tag on.

Entering the Classroom

Check on daily chore.

Eat breakfast.

Brush teeth.

Take money to "bank."

Talk with a friend.

Lunches

As children enter the classroom, have them immediately get rid of the extras they are carrying. A box for lunches is placed near the door. They may deposit the lunch box in the box before taking off coats, hats, mittens and boots. A large plastic or wicker laundry basket, a bushel basket or a large television box works well for lunch storage–something with two handles to let children carry it to the lunchroom at lunchtime.

Coats and Caps, Boots and Mittens

Have a special place for each child to put coats, caps, boots and mittens. Name tags hung on hooks serve two purposes: they identify the spot where coats are to be hung and they provide a place for name tags. Name tags are worn on the first few days of school, when substitute teachers are in the classroom, when parents assist with centers, when children go to other classrooms, when the class goes on field trips or for other activities.

Notes

Think about hanging an apron or smock with pockets on the wall in your classroom. Each pocket can be designed for a specific purpose. A pencil-shaped pocket holds pencils. A note pad pocket holds notes. A tape-shaped pocket holds tape.

As children enter the door, they can put their notes in the note pocket.

Baggage Claim

Provide a table for students to unpack book bags. This table should have organizing baskets or tubs for notes, completed work, completed corrections, etc.

Book Return

Children should become responsible for checking in their own library books when they are returned. Post library pockets on poster board. Provide a pocket for each child, with each child's name on the pocket. When library books are checked out, children should put their library card in their library pocket. When they return the book, they will get the library card from the chart pocket, place the card in the book's pocket and put the book on a book cart, ready for classroom use or return to the library.

Name Tags

At the beginning of the year and in unique situations, children need to wear name tags. Let them be responsible for those name tags. Plan a special spot for them: pin them to a special bulletin board, hang them on the children's coat hooks, decorate a name tag caddy or label a storage box.

It is each child's responsibility to wear the name tag when asked to: the first week of school, for a substitute, for the teacher, for the librarian or for parent volunteers.

Be careful about the use of name tags on field trips. Some feel it is safer not to have the name pinned to a child when in public places. If teachers feel students need to have some identification on them when they are on field trips or out on walks, pin on the name tag with the name toward the child's body and a decoration or the school's name facing out.

Sharing Board and/or Table

Provide a bulletin board where children can post things that they wish to share with others. A table in front or near the board allows children to place things for others to examine. If the object is a hands-off item, children should attach a red dot to warn others that they do not wish to have their item handled.

Sign In

To cut down on time for taking attendance, provide a place for children to "register" each day as they enter the room.

Provide a registration sheet with everyone's name. Each child should sign their name or write their initials in a column.

Write names on tongue depressors. Put the tongue depressor in card pockets on a chart designed to match the room theme. As children enter the room, they take their name stick out of the pocket on the chart and place the stick in a juice can. Use the names in the juice can to call on children during the day. This helps make sure that each child has a turn to respond. As each child is called on, give them their name sticks. As they leave the classroom, they return the name sticks to the attendance chart.

Register for Lunch

In schools where hot lunch is served, an accurate lunch count is necessary early in the day. This is another time teachers call each child's name–time consuming and a wait time for children. Either the time has to be eliminated or shortened. Have students sign up for lunch in the same way they do for attendance. Label each can for the type of lunch children want. Some of the older children can transfer the names to the official lunch report by placing an X near each child's name as they go through the names in the cans.

School Lunch

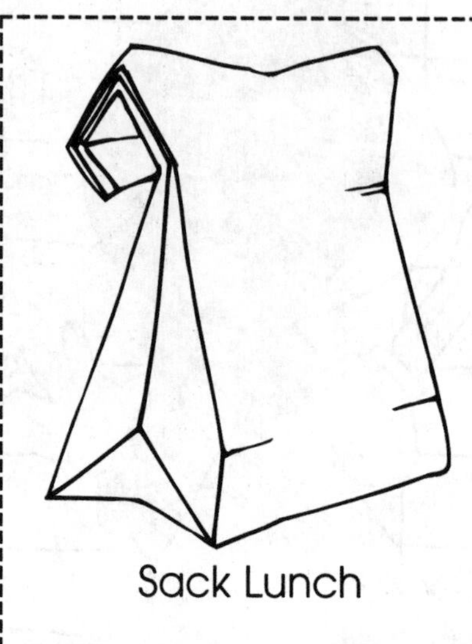

Sack Lunch

Going Home for Lunch

Register for Milk

Take the milk count the same way as the lunch count. Children take a name stick and place it in a white milk carton, a chocolate milk carton or a paper cup to indicate what they will have to drink with snack or lunch.

White Milk

Chocolate Milk

No Milk

Check on Daily Chores

When children enter the classroom, they should consider it their classroom. Because it is theirs, it is their responsibility to care for it. Take photographs of children doing different chores in the room. Place these photographs on theme or seasonal punch-outs, placing self-adhesive magnetic strips to the back, near the top of the punch-out. Ask children to help name each task. Write the name of the task on the punch-out. Place the strips on a metal board, a filing cabinet or pin to a bulletin board.

Each child has a name card that also has a self-adhesive magnetic strip attached to the back. The name cards are placed on the punch-out chore, held by the magnets. One of the tasks is to change the chore chart daily. Another task is to be a substitute for students who are absent. Try to make sure that each child has some responsibility each day. Or make buttons from the pictures on pages 61 to 68 and allow the children to wear the button for the task appropriate to the day. Make pictures in circles the size of circle button makers.

Entering the Classroom

Light Switcher

Entering the Classroom

Boys' Lunch Counter

Entering the Classroom

Boys' Line Caboose

Entering the Classroom

Girls' Line Caboose

Trash Collector

Gardener

Entering the Classroom

Milk Person

Paper Passer

Entering the Classroom

Entering the Classroom

Pet Handler

Entering the Classroom

Noise Controller

Entering the Classroom

Coat Monitor

Entering the Classroom

Pencil Sharpener

Paper Collector

Librarian

Napkin Folder

Straw Placer

Messenger

Entering the Classroom

Calendar

Entering the Classroom

Meteorologist

Entering the Classroom

Floor Monitor

Entering the Classroom

Block Monitor

Entering the Classroom

Puzzle Monitor

Art Center Monitor

Entering the Classroom

Tape Player

Entering the Classroom

Record Player

Entering the Classroom

Substitute

Entering the Classroom

Chore Changer

Entering the Classroom

Girls' Lunch Counter

Eat Breakfast

If children eat breakfast in your program, make sure they do as much of the preparation for themselves as they can. This prepares them to make breakfast for themselves at home, rather than depending on someone else. Instead of following breakfast with teeth brushing and circle time, direct them to go from eating to teeth brushing and on to working at the centers.

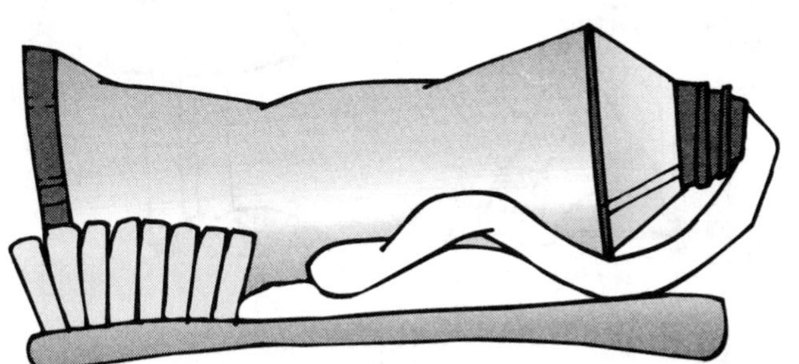

Brush Teeth

Health standards in the state govern tooth brushing time. For safety, store brushes separately and in a location that is open to the air. Because a common tube of toothpaste passes germs, tooth brushing with no paste is better than no brushing at all.

Sharpening Pencils

The pencil sharpener always seems to become a control issue for teachers. It could be the sound of grinding pencils, the movement of children in the room or possibly because children break leads so they can get up and move around (should tell us something). But children do need sharp pencils for daily work.

Choose from any one of these strategies:

- Allow children to sharpen pencils when they need to but allow only two children at the sharpener at a time.
- Have a can of sharpened and unsharpened pencils (all the same kind) available. When the lead gets too dull, allow children to go to the desk, place the dull pencil in one can and take a sharpened one to use. A helper may sharpen the pencils periodically during the day.
- Suggest children have a supply of five pencils. Schedule the sharpening to occur at specific times: before school, before and after recess and before and after lunch. Allow only four children to sharpen all five pencils at that time. It is hard to monitor and control this method.

Use the Restroom

Children must have a time to use the restroom before the day begins. Some may have been on the bus for an hour just after breakfast. Allow them to go as they need.

The best way to avoid the problems of wait time while the whole class goes to the restroom is to have a bathroom in your classroom which children are allowed to use as needed. Or allow children to use bathroom passes as needed as long as they are able to control their own behavior. If they are unable to do that, require them to go as a group with an adult supervisor, at the convenience of the adult (but at the necessity of the children).

Finish Homework

Allow children to complete their homework at school during the first few minutes while other routine procedures are taking place. If they cannot do their chores that morning, have them ask a friend to do their chore for them and say that they will return the favor. Being helpful is a good trait to acquire.

Talk with a Friend

Allow the children to talk a while before things get started. They will do it anyway and time will be spent trying to get them quiet. After they have had some time to socialize, ask that they remain quiet for the upcoming work time. They are then more likely to respect the rule.

Get Right to Work

Some children or groups of children have difficulty with the freedom that some of the above tasks allow. These children need to get right to work. Have them enter the room and get to work immediately on a task they find rewarding (not challenging, not boring). It may be a challenge to find the right set of tasks.

Switching Signals

Have a signal to warn children that only a short time is left before they must completely stop a task. Typically the only times this isn't done is during emergency situations. Also, a signal that tells students to stop what they are doing, clean up and move to the next activity or time of the day is important.

The signals listed are "attention getters." Teach students to respond to the appropriate signals.

"Boys and girls (alternate with girls and boys), I'd like to have your attention."

The best signal is a special phrase spoken in a normal tone of voice, "Girls and boys, I need your attention," at which point they are expected to get quiet so their teacher may speak. This signal seems the most realistic because it is how many people behave in the real world.

Tapping on a Glass

Everyone has attended a dinner where someone taps on a glass to get attention. This can also be used in the classroom at breakfast, snack or lunch. It is fairly realistic and something that children will probably hear again in their lives, a signal to listen to the speaker.

Bell Ring

A bell is a somewhat realistic signal, and something that may be seen or heard in the real world. When children hear the bell, they must be quiet. After they have learned the bell signal, ask students where else bells are used as a warning (train crossing, clock towers, fire alarms). The bell ringing can be a signal for students to get quiet or to move to the next activity.

Timer

Use a timer for relatively standard and sequential periods in the classroom. The timer is something students might be used to hearing. At home it signals a time to check the cooking to see if it is done. In the classroom it can signal a time for children to check their work to see if they are almost done and ready to move on. It could also signal a time to move to the next activity.

Basketball Bounce

Bounce a basketball to get students' attention. The noise is different from the noise in the room. Then tell them what they must do next. If the class sings or says a cleanup song, rhyme or rap, it can signal the rhythm.

Lights

In many classrooms teachers turn off the lights as a cue for children to quiet down and listen to an announcement. It is effective for most children because it is a visual cue when they are already involved in talking and moving.

In some classrooms a flick off and on of the lights is the signal to clean up and move on to the next activity.

Nursery Rhymes, Songs, Chants and Poems

On the following pages are names of nursery rhymes, songs, chants and poems. Included are ways they might be used as signals to switch. In addition, children can make books of the rhymes they know.

Nursery Rhymes, Songs, Chants and Poems

Post a set of nursery rhymes, songs, chants or poems in various spots in the room. Use them when it is time for students to stop what they are doing, chime in, clean up and move to the next activity. For example, nursery rhymes may be the cue to go from group time to centers; songs are the cue to clean up centers and get in line for recess; etc.

The pictures that follow may be copied, colored and posted. As a rhyme, song or poem is learned, take time to color the pictures and hang them up.

Periodically during the year or as they are learned, have the children color a copy of the rhymes, songs and poems that they know and put them in a book of Rhymes I Know. If students are old enough they can write a copy of the rhyme, song or poem to go along with the picture, using whatever invented spellings are needed.

Hey, Diddle, Diddle

Switching Signals
Rub a Dub Dub

Three Little Kittens

Switching Signals
Rain, Rain, Go Away

Switching Signals
Pussy Cat, Pussy Cat

Switching Signals
Pat a Cake

Switching Signals
Wee Willie Winkie

Switching Signals
To Market, to Market

Switching Signals

Diddle, Diddle, Dumpling
Switching Signals

Old King Cole
Switching Signals

Little Bo Peep
Switching Signals

Little Miss Muffet
Switching Signals

Little Jack Horner

Switching Signals

Jack Sprat

Jack Be Nimble

Switching Signals

There Was a Crooked Man

Switching Signals

Switching Signals

Peter, Peter, Pumpkin Eater

Switching Signals

Mistress Mary

Switching Signals

Georgie Porgie

Switching Signals

Hickety Pickety
My Black Hen

Songs We Know

Switching Signals

Songs I Know

London Bridge

Switching Signals

Three Blind Mice

Switching Signals

Ring Around the Rosie

Switching Signals

Sing a Song of Sixpence

Switching Signals

Twinkle, Twinkle, Little Star

Switching Signals

Little Bunny Foo Foo

The Ants Go Marching

If You're Happy and You Know It

Row, Row, Row Your Boat

Mary Had a Little Lamb

Switching Signals
ABCs

Switching Signals
Baa Baa Black Sheep

Switching Signals
There Were 10
in the Bed

Switching Signals
The Old Woman Who
Swallowed a Fly

Yankee Doodle

Switching Signals

Bear Went over the Mountain

Hot Cross Buns

Switching Signals

Rig-a-Jig-Jig

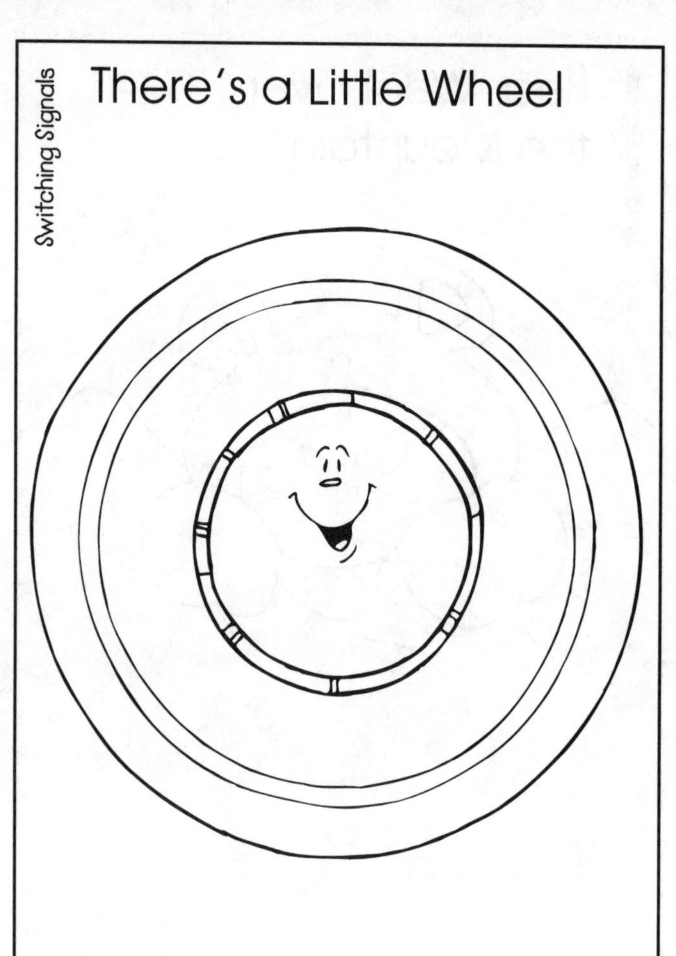
Switching Signals
There's a Little Wheel

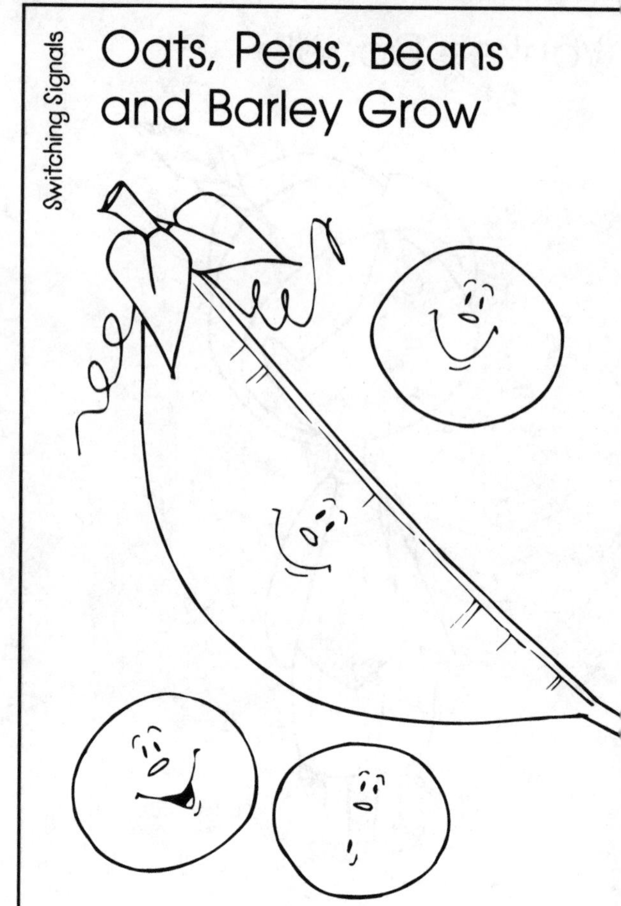
Switching Signals
Oats, Peas, Beans
and Barley Grow

Switching Signals
Love Somebody,
Yes I Do!

Switching Signals
Are You Sleeping?

Found a Peanut

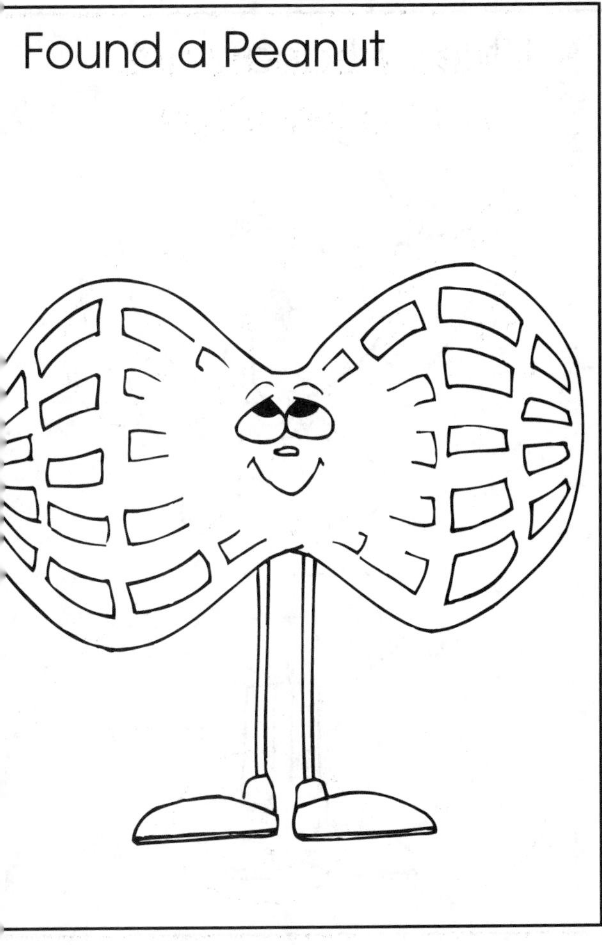

Switching Signals

Pop Goes the Weasel

It's Raining; It's Pouring

Switching Signals

Hickory, Dickory, Dock

Switching Signals

Eensy Weensy Spider

Switching Signals

Little Sir Echo

Switching Signals

Six Little Ducks That I Once Knew

Switching Signals

Down by the Station

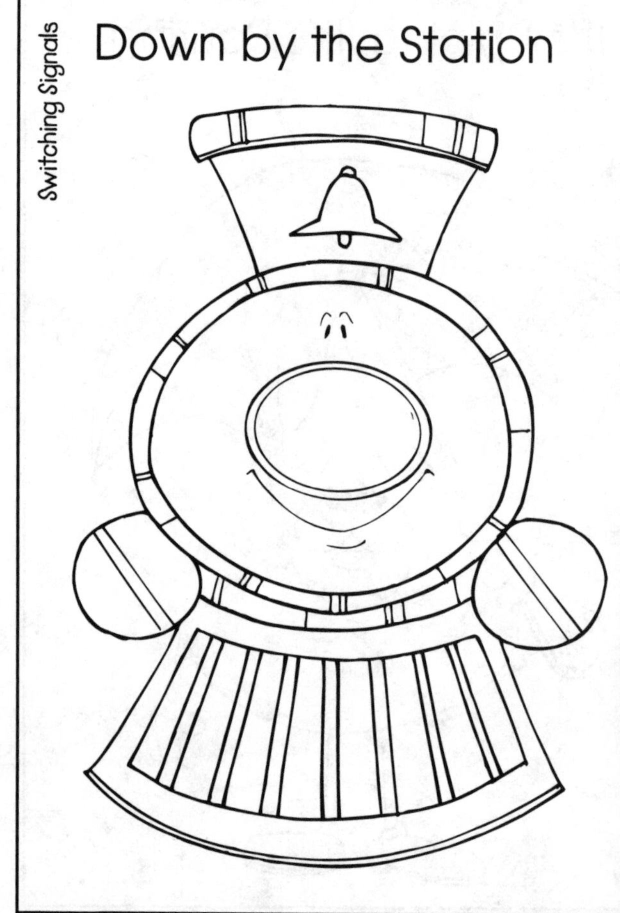

Poems and Chants We Know

Switching Signals

Poems and Chants I Know

Five Little Monkeys

Switching Signals

Teddy Bear, Teddy Bear

Switching Signals
Thirty Days Hath
September
September

Switching Signals
Shel Silverstein's
Pancake?

Switching Signals
Shel Silverstein's
Two Boxes

Switching Signals
Shel Silverstein's
Spaghetti

Action Songs

Cut out the Action Songs We Know card and post it near the large group gathering area. Below it or around it, post a list of action songs the children know or will learn. When students are involved in an activity and they should come to circle or large group time, go to the gathering area and sing action songs. In this way, children can clean up and come right to the area, join in the singing and be busy instead of sitting and waiting (and getting in trouble because they can't sit still).

Action Songs We Know

Action Songs I Know

Action Songs
Looby Loo

Action Songs
The Farmer in the Dell

Action Songs
This Is the Way We Wash Our Clothes

Action Songs
Hokey Pokey

Where Is Thumbkin?

Action Songs

This Little Piggy Went to the Market

The Wheels on the Bus

Action Songs

Head and Shoulders, Knees and Toes

Action Songs
The Noble Duke of York

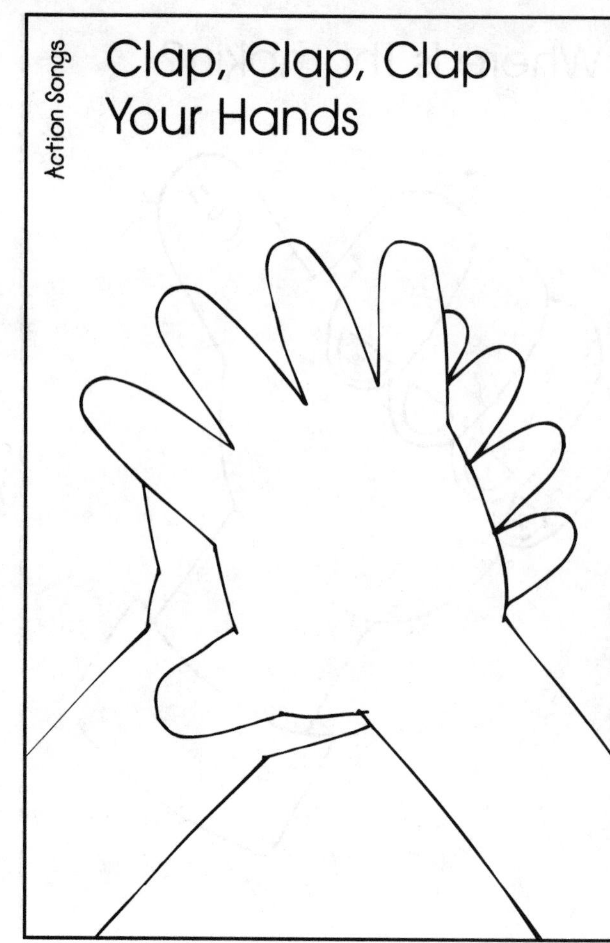
Action Songs
Clap, Clap, Clap
Your Hands

Action Songs
Did You Ever See a
Lassie/Laddie?

Action Songs
If You're Happy and
You Know It

Say It While You Work

Ready for Lunch Rap

It's *time* to clean the *room* and get ready for *lunch,*
We *do* a good *job,* 'cause we're the _____ *bunch.*

The *books* are on the *shelves* and the papers put *away,*
We *do* a good *job,* so we *don't* have to *stay.*

The *chairs* are pushed *in* all the *floor* is really *neat,*
We *do* a good *job* when it's *time* to go *eat.*
We *do* a good *job* when it's *time* to go *eat.*
We *do* a good *job* when it's *time* to go *eat.*

Kindergarten Is the Best

Learn the "Kindergarten Rap" from the movie *Kindergarten Cop.*

Whistle While You Work

Play and learn "Whistle While You Work" from the movie *Snow White.*

Transition Songs

Sing to the tune of "London Bridge Is Falling Down."

Put toys away and come to circle time.

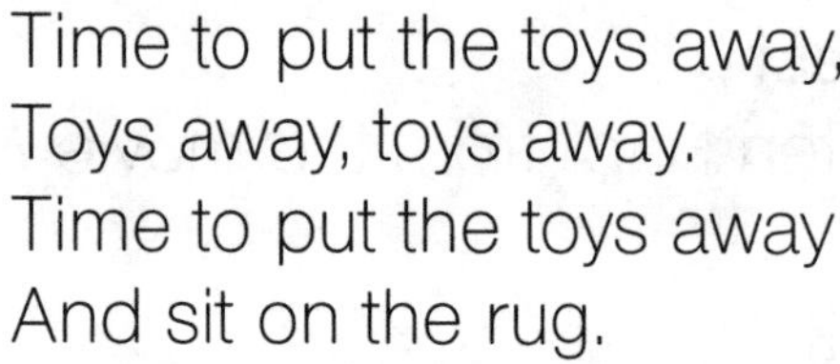

Time to put the toys away,
Toys away, toys away.
Time to put the toys away
And sit on the rug.

Time to put the toys away,
Alex, Anne, Molly, Sam.
Time to put the toys away
And sit on the rug.

Put toys away and line up at the door.

Time to put the toys away,
Toys away, toys away.
Time to put the toys away
And line up at the door.

Put toys away and get coats on.

Time to put the toys away,
Toys away, toys away.
Time to put the toys away
And put on your coats.

Sing to the tune of "The Wheels on the Bus."

Pick Up Time

Children in the room are pickin' up,
Pickin' up, pickin' up.
Children in the room are pickin' up,
And puttin' things away.

Helen's in the room and pickin' up,
Pickin' up, pickin' up.
Orville's in the room and pickin' up
And puttin' things away.

Girls in the room are pickin' up,
Pickin' up, pickin' up.
Boys in the room are pickin' up
And puttin' things away.

Good Morning Song

Good morning to you,
Good morning to you.
We're all in our places
With sunshining faces.
Oh, this is the way
We start every day.

Poems

Sit down at circle time

Teddy Bear, Teddy Bear,
Touch your toes.
Teddy Bear, Teddy Bear,
Touch your nose.
Teddy Bear, Teddy Bear,
Turn around.
Teddy Bear, Teddy Bear,
Sit right down.

Keep your hands to yourselves

I have ten little fingers
That all belong to me.
I make them do a lot of things
Would you like to see?

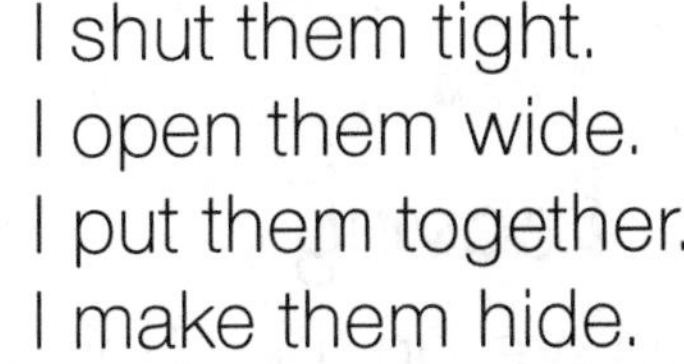

I shut them tight.
I open them wide.
I put them together.
I make them hide.

I make them go high.
I make them go low.
I fold them up tight.
And hold them just so.

For rest time

In school when the days are hot
I like to find a quiet spot
And hardly move a single bit
And sit, and sit, and sit, and sit.

Sing to the tune of "The Farmer in the Dell."

Find a spot and rest

The toys are all away.
The books have all been read.
It's time to find a quiet spot,
And go quietly to bed.

Leaving

The toys are on the shelves.
The papers put away.
It's time to line up at the door.
Because we cannot stay.

Sing to the tune of "Hot Cross Buns."

Get ready for a story.

Sit right down.
Sit right down.
Sit right down and fold your legs.
Listen to the book.

Get in line.

Get in line.
Get in line.
Get in line, hands at sides.
Face the front.

Indoor recess (rain)

It's raining outside.
It's raining outside.
We'll work inside and play inside.
It's raining outside.

Indoor recess (snow)

It's snowing outside.
It's snowing outside.
We'll work inside and play inside.
It's snowing outside.

Sing to the tune of "Here We Go 'Round the Mulberry Bush."

Put the toys away and go home.

This is the way we pick up the toys,
Pick up the toys, pick up the toys.
This is the way we pick up the toys
And get ready to go home.

Hang up coats and get right to work.

This is the way we hang up coats.
Hang up coats, hang up coats.
This is the way we hang up coats,
And sit right down to work.

Sing to the tune of "Here We Go 'Round the Mulberry Bush."

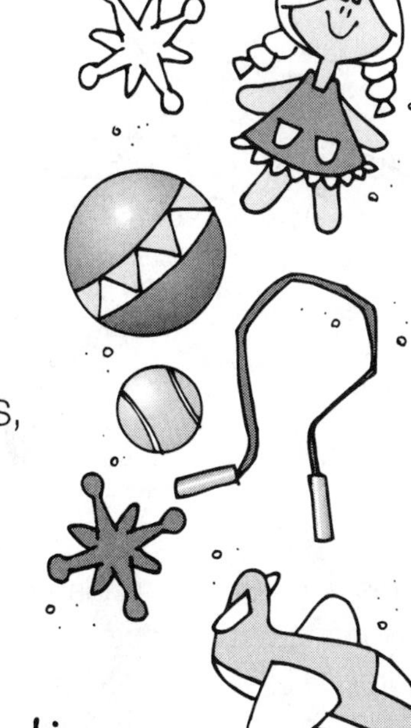

Put the toys away.

This is the way we pick up the toys,
Pick up the toys, pick up the toys.
This is the way we pick up the toys
And put them all away.

José and Beth help pick up the toys,
Pick up the toys, pick up the toys.
Ali and Jim help pick up the toys
And put them all away.

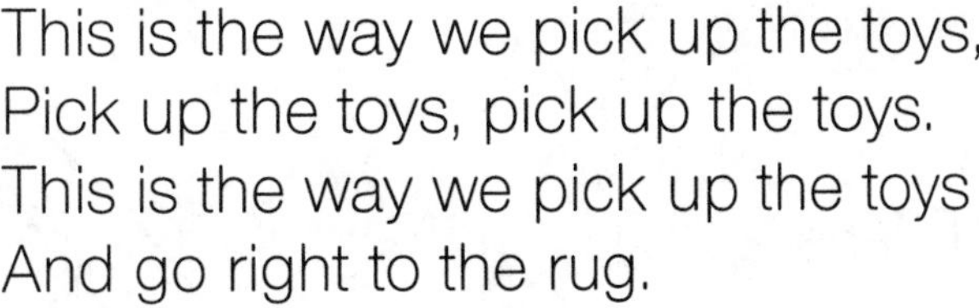

Put the toys away and go to circle time.

This is the way we pick up the toys,
Pick up the toys, pick up the toys.
This is the way we pick up the toys
And go right to the rug.

Put the toys away and line up at the door.

This is the way we pick up the toys,
Pick up the toys, pick up the toys.
This is the way we pick up the toys
And line up at the door.

Put the toys away and go outside.

This is the way we pick up the toys,
Pick up the toys, pick up the toys.
This is the way we pick up the toys
And get ready to go outside.

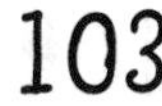

What Next?

It is very difficult to plan just the right amount of time for children to complete an activity. This is why working with objects and investigating real and meaningful things are the best ways to help young children. However, there are times when some children don't want to do what is there or who complete a task and need something else to do. Here are some suggestions to answer the question, "What can I do now?"

Fun-Filled Fillers

Provide children with a list of activities from which to choose (pages 105-107). When they decide on one activity, they place a check in the box and date the activity. When their sheet is filled, they can get another one. The activities should be available for them to complete at their convenience.

Rather than providing students with sheets of their own to fill out, post one activity or one of the sheets daily.

Activities provided on pages 105-107 are also provided on pages 108-128. Place these in a box in the room where children can go to select one when they are finished with other things they are doing. Make duplicates so more than one student can do the same activity.

Spare Time Specials

Make or do a crossword puzzle.

Color or draw a picture.

Play a game of cards with a friend.

Read or listen to a story.

Make or do a word search.

Draw or build a model.

Construct or draw an animal.

signature

Spare Time Specials

- ❑ Write a recipe for your favorite pizza.
- ❑ Write a letter.
- ❑ Design a feely bag.
- ❑ Make a list of things in your desk.
- ❑ Trace or draw your hands or feet.
- ❑ Design a new pair of shoes.
- ❑ Tape a commercial for your favorite candy.

signature

Spare Time Specials

- ❑ Weigh and record each thing in your desk.
- ❑ Take and record your pulse rate for one minute. Jump in place. Take and record your pulse again.
- ❑ Write a verse to "Roses Are Red."
- ❑ List the famous people you know.
- ❑ Toss and catch a spongy ball.
- ❑ Make a fuzzy bunny.
- ❑ Graph your classmates' shoe types.

signature

Spare Time Specials

- ❑ Make a wish list for you or a frie
- ❑ Draw things that come in threes
- ❑ Measure and record each thing in your desk.
- ❑ What do you see out the windo
- ❑ Draw or write about how to recycle.
- ❑ Jump rope.
- ❑ Design a new car.

signature

Spare Time Specials

Stitch a pattern onto burlap.

Draw a map to your friend's house.

Construct a model city.

Write a poem about yourself.

Describe your favorite dance.

Thank your favorite author.

Do a puzzle.

signature

Spare Time Specials

- ❑ Make a list of ball players.
- ❑ Make a list of singers.
- ❑ Clean your desk or cubby.
- ❑ Read a book.
- ❑ Read a book with a friend.
- ❑ Write the story of your favorite movie.
- ❑ Make a hard spelling list.

signature

- [ ] Make or do a crossword puzzle.

- [ ] Color or draw a picture.

❑ Play a game of cards with a friend.

❑ Read or listen to a story.

❑ Make or do a word search.

❑ Draw or build a model.

❑ Construct or draw an animal.

❑ Write a recipe for your favorite pizza.

❑ Write a letter.

❑ Design a feely bag.

❑ Make a list of things in your desk.

❑ Trace or draw your hands or feet.

❑ Design a new pair of shoes.

❑ Tape a commercial for your favorite candy.

❑ Weigh and record each thing in your desk.

❑ Take and record your pulse rate for one minute. Jump in place. Take and record your pulse rate again.

❑ Write a verse to "Roses Are Red."

❑ List the famous people you know.

❑ Toss and catch a spongy ball.

❑ Make a fuzzy bunny.

❑ Graph your classmates' shoe types.

❑ Make a wish list for you or a friend.

three 3 3 3 three 3 3 3 three 3 3 THREE 3 3 3 3 three 3 3 3 3 3 3 three 3 3

❑ Draw things that come in threes.

❑ Measure and record each thing in your desk.

❑ What do you see out the window?

REUSE Recycle

❑ Draw or write about how to recycle.

rethink

Recycle refuse

❑ Jump rope.

❑ Design a new car.

❑ Stitch a pattern onto burlap.

❑ Draw a map to your friend's house.

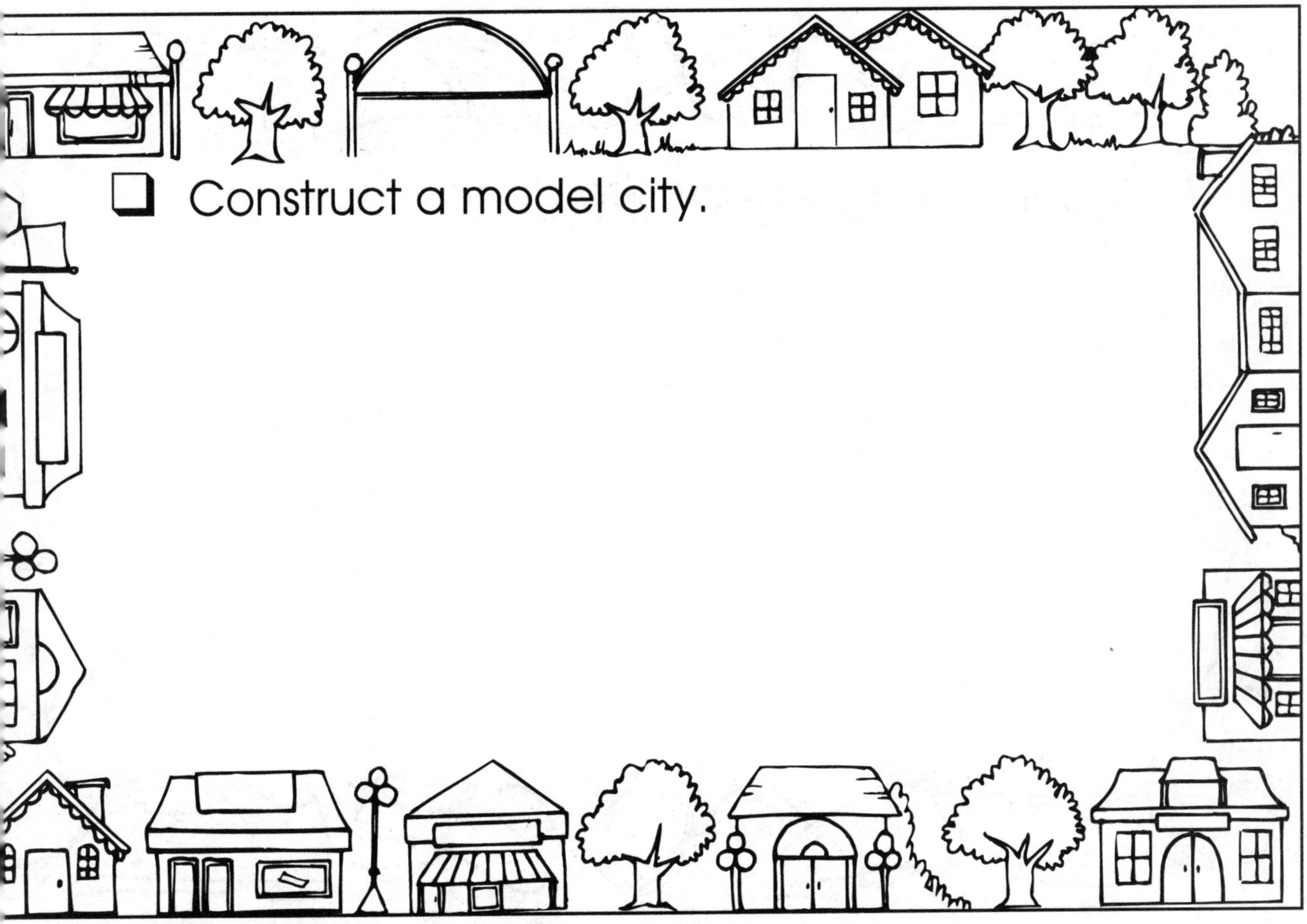

❑ Construct a model city.

❑ Write a poem about yourself.

❑ Describe your favorite dance.

❑ Thank your favorite author.

❑ Do a puzzle.

❑ Make a list of ball players.

❑ Make a list of singers.

❑ Clean your desk or cubby.

❑ Read a book.

❑ Read a book with a friend.

❑ Write the story of your favorite movie.

❑ Make a hard spelling list.

School Breaks

Keep Learning Alive During School Breaks

Transitions occur as children leave school for periodic breaks, one to two days in length (Martin Luther King, Jr. Day; Presidents' Day; Memorial Day; Fourth of July; Labor Day; Thanksgiving) or longer breaks (spring break, summer break, fall break, winter break). Homework assignments during this time are not necessary and many times turn off both students and parents. There are better ways to help children and parents *keep learning alive during school breaks.*

Sharing Board

When children travel during school breaks (amusement parks, favorite eating establishments, the lake, short trips, long trips), ask them to bring something back to share. As children look to see what other children have done, they are reading objects, artifacts and actual words.

Journals for Break

The following pages are blank pages for the children to use during breaks to record what they do. Send one home over break with the following note attached:

Dear Parents,

Please place this sheet on your refrigerator or in another safe place. Work with your child to record what you do during this break from school. Include TV, playing with friends, taking long naps, swimming, eating out, vacationing. Record these activities on the Journal Sheet provided by using pictures, menus, sacks, logos or words. Return the sheet on the next school day to place on our Sharing Board.

Summer Fun

Parents and children alike look forward to doing something special. Many times a child's first question of the day is "What are we going to do today?" Sometimes parents can't think of another fun thing to do.

Provide parents with a calendar of activities to share with their children. Send the June calendar home on the last day of school. Mail the July calendar at the end of June and August calendar at the end of July. Attach a brief note to keep families connected to school.

Dear ______________________________,

How's your summer going? I cleaned up our classroom and put all the things away for next year. Since then I have just enjoyed my family. We have gone swimming and to the movies. Once we went to play miniature golf.

I have sent a calendar along for this month. It has some new things you can do. Have you been playing? Have you been watching TV? What interesting books have you read? Write and tell me. My address is

____

____

Have some more summer fun!

Sincerely,

____

signature

June

Sunday	Monday	Tuesday	Wednesday	Thursday	Friday	Saturday
	Walk around the block. Count the houses. What shapes are the windows?	Plan a special Sunday meal.	Trace each family member's shoes. Decorate.	Record your favorite family stories.	Soak beans in water overnight.	Check beans. What's happening?
Read the comics together.	Dip popcorn in cheese, salt, cinnamon, pepper, sugar.	Make an ABC book of things that are in your house.	Make signs for each family member's door.	Draw chalk animals on the driveway or sidewalk.	Make hot chocolate. Melt ice cube in it. Drink.	Plant some flower seeds.
Draw chalk shapes on driveway. Bounce balls to them.	Make a list of things that come in threes.	See which foods are crunchy and which are soft.	Visit an art museum.	Look at old photographs together.	Find where your relatives live on a map.	Make a list of the names of soups off the cans. Label your favorite.
ind interesting pictures in nagazines.	Draw a self-portrait. Hang it on the refrigerator.	Draw pictures of animals you like.	Read each family member's favorite story.	Design magnets using magnetic strips, glue, paper, glitter.	Draw a chalk highway. Travel it with toy cars.	Make flowers out of pipe cleaners and tissue paper.
ake a nagnifying lass walk.	Play your favorite game.	Listen to your favorite tape or watch your favorite video.				

July

Sunday	Monday	Tuesday	Wednesday	Thursday	Friday	Saturday
	Find a map of your state and locate points of interest.	Look for traffic signs as you travel.	Make a tent out of a blanket and lawn chairs. Have a picnic.	Make a flag cake using white icing, strawberries and blueberries.	Read *The Noisy Cricket.* Find some and listen to them.	Pick out fresh fruits at the fruit market.
Pull weeds out of your garden.	Find your favorite book at the library.	Play Frisbee™ with plastic lids.	Take out all the pots and pans. Match them. Clean cupboard.	Draw pictures on coffee filters with markers.	Read *It Looked Like Spilt Milk.* Look at the clouds.	Tie steamers to your bike and take a ride with friends.
Make bracelets and necklaces with string and macaroni.	Go to a movie with your family.	Play hop-scotch.	Make a para-chute. Use napkin, string, paper clips.	Play in the sand with funnels and strainers.	How many times can you bounce a ball? Count and tally.	Pull your stuffed ani-mals in a wagon.
Sit under an umbrella in the sprinkler. Catch water off the edges.	Collect water-melon seeds and make a picture of them.	Draw a chalk family on your driveway.	Make a paper cup sculpture.	Make alu-minum foil boats. Float them outside.	Put salt in a cake pan. Draw pictures.	Dress up your stuffed ani-mals in your clothes.
Read Eric Carle's book about light-ning bugs.	Catch lightning bugs in a jar. Then let them go free.	Exercise with your family.	Fill cans that have lids with rice and sand. make noise outside.			

August

Sunday	Monday	Tuesday	Wednesday	Thursday	Friday	Saturday
	Sort through a drawer and clean it out.	Make chalk drawings	Place jelly on sidewalk near ants and watch what happens.	Run through the sprinkler with your rain-coat on.	Go to the library.	Shoot news-paper balls into a trash can.
it in the yard nd draw a icture of your avorite tree. rame it with raft sticks.	Look for insects. Name them or find out about them in books.	Use cups, straws, hoses and ladles with water in pails.	Build a bridge with boxes and sticks.	Make and play with play-dough.	Decorate a grocery sack. Take it to the store for gro-ceries.	Take a family walk and count all the animals you see.
inger-paint utside in our bathing uit. Use our hands nd feet.	Make a list of friends and their phone numbers.	Play concentration.	Paint the side-walk and steps with water and paint brushes.	Watch TV show together as a family.	Bake a cake.	Find school supplies in the newspaper. Price them at different stores.
ead some ursery hymes ogether.	Collect dirt, twigs, sticks and string. Try to make a bird's nest.	Name all your stuffed ani-mals. Make name tags for them.	Visit your school.	Make a sticker picture.	Make your grocery list on a paper sack. Use the sack at the grocery store.	Find some free enter-tainment in the newspa-per. Try it.
lake fruit uice ice cubes.	Find all the plastic stor-age contain-ers and match them with lids.	Make shape sandwiches for lunch with cookie cut-ters.	Dip apples slices in vari-ous things: peanut butter, honey, jelly, yogurt, etc.			

Further Reading

Boyer, Ernest. *The Basic School: A Community for Learning.* Princeton, NJ: The Carnegie Foundation for the Advancement of Teaching, 1995.

Bredekamp, S. (Ed.). *Developmentally Appropriate Practice in Early Childhood Program Serving Children From Birth Through Age 8.* Washington, D.C.: NAEYC, 1987.

Charney, R.S., and M.K. Clayton, "The First 6 Weeks of School: Building the Foundation for a Successful Year." *The Responsive Classroom,* 6(2). Greenfield, MA: Northeast Foundation for Children, 1994, Fall/Winter.

Emmer, E.T., C.M. Evertson, L.M. Anderson. "Effective Classroom Management at the Beginning of the School Year." In Doyle, W., and T.L. Good. (Eds.). *Focus on Teaching: Readings from the Elementary School Journal.* Chicago, IL: The University of Chicago Press, 1982.

Love, J.M., and M.E. Logue. *Transitions to Kindergarten in American Schools: Final Report of the National Transition Study.* Portsmouth, NH: Research Corporation, 1992.